SEWING
MACHINE
EMBROIDERY
AND STITCHERY

SEWING MACHINE EMBROIDERY AND STITCHERY

TECHNIQUES, INSPIRATION, AND PROJECTS FOR
EMBROIDERY, APPLIQUÉ, QUILTING,
PATCHWORK, AND TRAPUNTO

by Thelma R. Newman
Lee Scott Newman
Jay Hartley Newman

CROWN PUBLISHERS, INC.
NEW YORK

Inquiries should be addressed to Crown Publishers, Inc., One Park
Avenue, New York, New York 10016

Printed in the United States of America

Published simultaneously in Canada by General Publishing Company
Limited

Library of Congress Cataloging in Publication Data

Newman, Thelma R.
  Machine embroidery and stitchery.

  Bibliography: p.
  Includes index.
    1. Machine sewing.   2. Needlework.   I. Newman,
Lee Scott, joint author.   II. Newman, Jay Hartley,
joint author.   III. Title.
TT713.N48 1980   746.44   80-11620

ISBN: 0-517-53214X (cloth)
      0-517-532518 (paper)

Designed by Deborah Kerner

10 9 8 7 6 5 4 3 2 1

First Edition

CONTENTS

ACKNOWLEDGMENTS

The help and encouragement of the many contributors to this book made it what it is. Our deepest appreciation goes to them:

Sydel Ackerman
Andrea Aldredge
Mary Ball
Jane Bearman
Joan Blumenbaum
Tina Bobker
Gloria L. Bubeck
Blanche Carstenson
Sas Colby
Charles Counts
Margaret Cusack
Niloofer Daver
Lenore Davis
Carol Dlugasch
Sara Drower
Saul Frances
Elizabeth S. Gurrier
The Handworks Gallery
Diane Herrick-Kvistad
Ellen Tobey Holmes

Becky King
Janet Kuemmerlein
Doreen Lah
Barbara F. Lambert
Sally Miller
Marcia Morse
Mountain Artisans
Pace Gallery
Anna V. A. Polesný
Rainbow Artisans, Inc.
Bets Ramsey
Ann Reilly
Rising Fawn Quilters
Lucas Samaras
Joy Saville
Joan Schulze
Josephine Schwartz
The Singer Co.
Sandra Ward

As always, Norm Smith did a superlative job of photo-processing, for which we are grateful; and our appreciation goes to Barbara J. Harr for typing the manuscript.

But our debt is greatest to Ann Reilly, then a student at the Fashion Institute of Technology, who was dedicated in assisting Thelma R. Newman, executed many of the pieces designed for this book, and was unsparing in providing us with the technical information necessary to complete it.

Our appreciation to Connie Joy Newman for her support in this undertaking. And, never least, our profound thanks to our father, Jack Newman.

NOTE: Photography by the authors unless otherwise credited.

PREFACE

The idea for this book was conceived originally by Thelma R. Newman early in 1978. She perceived that even as the first portable sewing machines had revolutionized traditional embroidery by making machine embroidery possible, electronic sewing machines would make machine embroidery a more exciting and expressive medium. She thought of this book as an instrument by which to fully and systematically explore the potential of the sewing machine as a means for decorating and constructing fabric. Toward that end, she designed and executed many of the pieces illustrated in this book. She also collected examples of some of the finest, most creative, and best designed work being executed by contemporary artists who work with fabrics and sewing machines.

For Thelma R. Newman, our mother, the period during which this book was conceived was, however, an extremely difficult one. She was afflicted with an illness which caused her death before she was able to finish writing it. In completing what would have been her twenty-first book on a wide range of arts, crafts, and other topics, we have tried to meet the high standards that she set for herself. We have tried as well to make this book as close as possible to what we understood her original conception of it to be. Perhaps the best preface is part of what Thelma R. Newman said in prefacing another book dealing with the uses and design of fabric forms, *Quilting, Patchwork, Appliqué, and Trapunto:*

> [F]abric is always fabric. It is never made to look like another material, such as glass or wood. Because fabric does not masquerade as something that it is not, fabric forms have an intrinsic validity. But we do come across examples of very bad design with fabric, particularly when old, hackneyed designs are slavishly and repeatedly copied. My personal preference is for original, contemporary design, using contemporary fabrics and techniques. I am not very tolerant of work that pretends to be of another era. This is no apology, but the motivation behind all my writing. High design standards are not difficult to maintain if we reflect ourselves, our styles of living and our environment.

JAY HARTLEY NEWMAN
LEE SCOTT NEWMAN

SEWING MACHINE EMBROIDERY AND STITCHERY

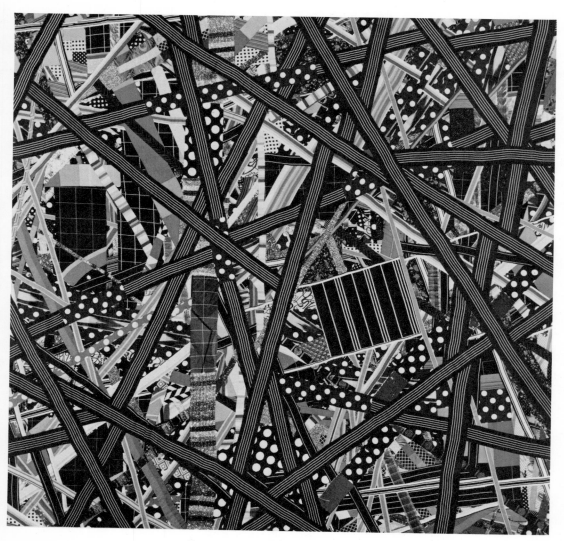

Reconstruction #31 (1977, 91¼″ x 101½″), by Lucas Samaras, is a collage of machine-sewn fabrics. *Courtesy: Pace Gallery, photo by Al Mozell*

1

INTRODUCTION

Machine embroidery was originally a commercial, industrial process made possible by machines that were invented and perfected during the nineteenth century. The machine that made machine embroidery possible was developed by Isaac Singer during the 1850s. It was employed almost exclusively by manufacturers for many years primarily to imitate fine hand embroidery. It was not until The Singer Company introduced the first portable electric sewing machine in the 1920s that machine embroidery became widely popular. Home needleworkers soon discovered this vehicle for the expression of individual creative energies. For the first time, home needleworkers could work directly with a tool that not only produced high-quality stitches, but did so extremely quickly.

The combination of quality, speed, and widespread use caused the unique decorative potential of the sewing machine to be explored rapidly. That exploration had an impact not only upon design but upon the development of successive generations of sewing machines, too. Contemporary sewing machines are, in many ways, extremely similar to those of the 1920s. But

1

A machine-embroidered
pendant by Joan Schulze.
Courtesy: Joan Schulze

In Trangression (1964, 18″ x 22″). Here Bets Ramsey combined appliqué and straight stitching. The free embroidery
straight stitching is in bright reds. Shadowy figures appear in
the foreground. *Courtesy: Bets Ramsey, Collection of I. D. Orr*

Machine-embroidered suede
and machine lace by Anna V.
A. Polesný. *Courtesy: Anna V.
A. Polesný*

A machine-appliquéd dress by Mountain Artisans. *Courtesy: Mountain
Artisans*

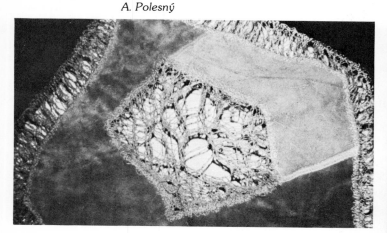

many new machines now offer a wider variety of stitches, adjustments, and accessories. As a result, the variations possible when using contemporary machines seem infinite. That range has influenced needleworkers to use their machines in innovative ways.

Today, machine embroidery is much more than the two-dimensional combination of thread and fabric. Appliqué, cording, faggoting, lace, quilting, and trapunto can be done by machine, with or without hand-embroidery additions. Because of the machine's speed, needleworks have grown in size. Pieces may still be wonderfully intricate and finely worked, but speed has brought the creation of ambitious monumental works within the realm of possibility.

The quality of a single machine-stitched line is different from that of handwork. Do not be fooled into inappropriate comparisons of the two. Each medium has its virtues and limitations. In combination, hand and machine are an incomparable team.

Alfonzo (8″ x 10″), one in a series of clown bags in machine-embroidered and -appliquéd suede by Anna V. A. Polesný. *Courtesy: Anna V. A. Polesný*

Joan Blumenbaum's *Open Wide*, free embroidered and appliquéd by machine and stuffed from behind in the trapunto technique.

Fantasy Garden, a suede vest free-embroidered in brightly colored silk threads by Anna V. A. Polesný. *Courtesy: Anna V. A. Polesný*

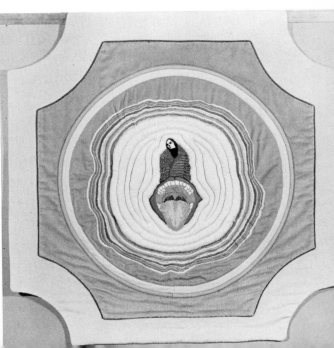

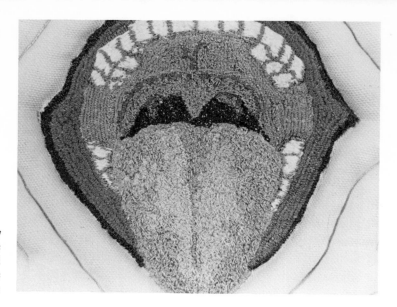

A close-up of *Open Wide* by Joan Blumenbaum showing the textures created by hand and machine embroidery. *Photos courtesy Joan Blumenbaum*

THE VARIABLES

To create machine embroidery, a working knowledge of the capabilities of your sewing machine is essential. The best way to begin is by re-reading the machine's instruction manual. Focus on the many ways in which the size and quality of the stitches may be varied. To develop skill in using the machine, practice manipulating the controls, changing stitch length, width, and tension. Such adjustments are extremely important in producing variety in machine stitchery. Consider some of the factors that will have a significant impact on the finished piece:

- Choice of *design;*
- Choice of *fabric* on which to work the design—its texture, pattern, color, and reflectance;
- Choice of *threads* with which to execute the project—their color, gloss, and thickness;
- *Stitches* to be used—and their length, width, and tension;
- *Speed:* most people work at medium speed, with an even pace;
- *Needles* should be compatible with fabric and thread (see chart, page 5);
- *Machine accessories,* such as various machine feet and needle plates, can be interchanged as required.

4

FABRIC TYPE

Delicate: chiffon, lace, organza, velvet

Lightweight: batiste, brocade, chiffon velvet, crepe, organdy, plastic film, ribbon, satin, shantung, silk, taffeta, voile

Medium weight: challis, chintz, corduroy (fine), faille, gingham, madras, percale, linen, suitings, seersucker, terry cloth, twill

Medium heavy: bonded fabrics, coatings, deep-pile fabrics, corduroy, drapery fabrics, duck, denim, gabardine, sailcloth, tweed, vinyl

Heavy: canvas, overcoatings, upholstery fabrics

Knits: double knits, bonded knits, ciré tricot, nylon tricot, spandex, jersey, stretch terry

Leather: calf, capeskin, buckskin, patent, lined leathers, simulated leathers, kidskin, suede

Vinyls (knit backing): suede, imitation leathers, crinkle patent, patent, embossed, printed

THREAD	NEEDLE SIZE
fine polyester, nylon, cotton	9*
cotton-wrapped polyester, 100 percent polyester (fine), 50 mercerized cotton, "A" nylon, "A" silk	11
cotton-wrapped polyester, 100 percent polyester, 50 mercerized cotton, 60 cotton, "A" silk	14
cotton-wrapped polyester, 100 percent polyester, heavy-duty mercerized cotton, 40–60 cotton	16
cotton-wrapped polyester, heavy-duty mercerized cotton, 40 cotton	18
cotton-wrapped polyester, 100 percent polyester, "A" nylon, "A" silk, 50 mercerized cotton	14
cotton-wrapped polyester, 100 percent polyester, 50 mercerized cotton, "A" nylon, "A" silk	11 14 16
cotton-wrapped polyester, 100 percent polyester, 50 mercerized cotton, "A" nylon, "A" silk	14

* The size 9 needle should be used only for sewing; use a larger needle for winding bobbins.

To get the most pleasure out of machine embroidery, work in an environment that is convenient and comfortable. There should be plenty of light, preferably some daylight. Many people prefer to sit in a comfortable, straight chair. An ironing board and iron should be handy. Maintain a clean area for arranging fabric and patterns and for cutting material. A few boxes for collecting scraps of fabric, yarn, and odds and ends become a ready source of supply for materials employed in appliqué. Try to stock a variety of threads—synthetics, silks, cottons, and the like—in a variety of thicknesses and colors. Easy access to scissors, bobbins, and other supplies will also make sewing more pleasant and efficient.

THE MACHINE

The sewing machine is the main tool of this craft and, if properly maintained, will serve well. Keep it free of dust, and oil it according to manufacturer's instructions. Never force it. Try to avoid hit-and-run accidents with straight pins. Learn about the special attachments that come with or are available for your machine. Many such devices are particularly useful in creating machine embroidery. Such equipment may include special feet, plates, and gauges.

The brand of machine that you use is not critical, as long as you are familiar with what your machine can and cannot do. Some machines are clearly capable of doing many more stitches, are easier to work with, and are more reliable than others. At a minimum, it is helpful to have a machine that can produce a zigzag stitch. Zigzag has become the most popular stitch for everything from satin-stitched monograms to appliqué. If your machine is fairly new and capable of semiautomatic or automatic stitching, learn to make the fullest possible use of such features. Some machines such as the Touch-Tronic 2000 (formerly the Athena 2000) and

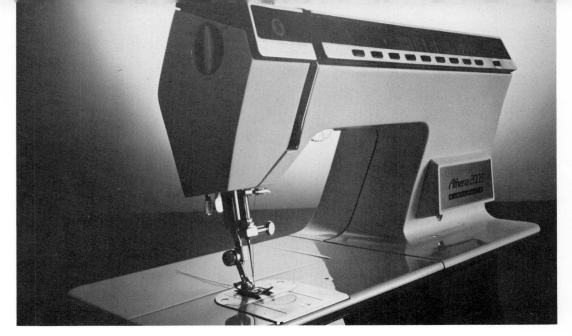

The Singer Company developed the first electronic home sewing machines: the Touch-Tronic 2000 (formerly the Athena 2000) and the Touch-Tronic 2001. Their electronic circuitry, single chips that contain over 8,000 transitions, replaced over 350 mechanical parts, including the elaborate cam systems that had previously been required to create complex patterns of stitches. Most of the work created for this book was executed on the Touch-Tronic 2000, an extraordinarily responsive and versatile machine. *Courtesy: The Singer Company*

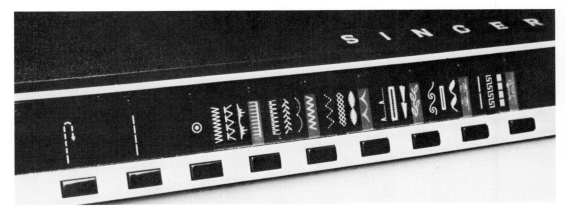

A close-up of the Touch-Tronic 2000 by Singer shows the panel through which stitch selection is controlled. Stitch patterns may be selected by simply pressing a button. *Courtesy: The Singer Company*

A close-up of the control panel of the Touch-Tronic 2001 shows that even the buttons have been eliminated. The panel, which is sensitive to the touch and "remembers" the settings that are selected, may be used to select the stitch and its length, width, and balance as well. *Courtesy: The Singer Company*

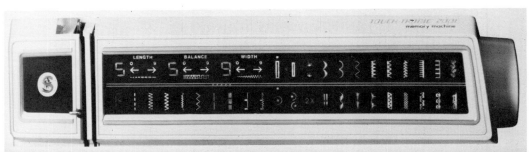

This elaborate sewing center developed by Singer suggests one possible arrangement of sewing machine, work space, accessories, threads, and other supplies. *Courtesy: The Singer Company*

the Touch-Tronic 2001, by the Singer Company, are programmed to sew more than twenty-five different stitches and to allow the operator to change from stitch to stitch at the touch of a button. You might never use some of the stitches possible on machines such as the Touch-Tronic 2000 and the Touch-Tronic 2001, but the majority of programmed stitch patterns will offer exciting design possibilities. A special stitch itself will often suggest design ideas. Chapter 2 presents the basic stitches and a vocabulary built on those basics.

Most of the machine stitching in this book has been done on a Singer Touch-Tronic 2000. It is a reliable machine and one adaptable to the many demands of machine embroidery, with many unique features. Nonetheless, first-rate results in machine embroidery can be readily achieved with machines that are not as elaborately conceived. Because each machine is slightly different, we will not discuss the peculiarities of any machine, nor will we dwell upon the precise settings of controls that adjust stitch width, length, and tension, as these are found on virtually every model. Consult the instruction booklet or a company representative if you have specific questions about the operation of a particular machine. Experimentation is the byword in learning to use your machine and in creating machine embroidery. It is the best way to determine what works and how to achieve different effects.

MACHINE ACCESSORIES

NEEDLES

Machine needles are available in a variety of sizes. The needle most commonly used is a size 12 (80). A fine fabric, such as a fine cotton organza, merits a finer needle, such as a size 10 (70). The needle should be matched to the fabric and thread. Use the *Needle Size* chart on page 5 for guidance in selecting the correct needle size. Where possible, use needles made for your machine, and always keep a range of sizes on hand.

Special needles are also available. Needles made for sewing leather, for example, have a triangular point and a longer, sharper cutting edge. Others influence the design of needlework, needles such as the wing needle, which makes large holes that become part of the decoration of fine fabrics. For needles, plates, feet, and other accessories, a visit to the local manufacturer's representative is often helpful.

Twin needles are another useful decorating tool. Twin stitching may be used to add a handsome finished look as top stitching. Twin needles are also used for pin-tucking. Experiment with thread tension. In pin-tucking, the upper tension is kept tight, so that the tightness pulls the fabric up in a little pin-tuck between the needles and imparts an interesting texture to the fabric. With twin needles, threads of different colors can be used, too. Consult the manual for your machine to see

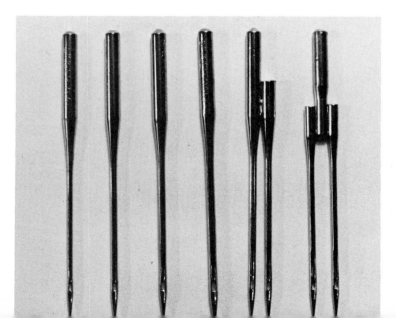

A variety of types and sizes of needles are available for different applications. For example, the twin needles at the far right would produce rows of stitching more widely separated than those that would be produced by the twin needles second from the right.

9

how this is done. Machine embroidery done in twin is double the embroidery. When embroidering in twin, be careful not to make the stitches too wide, or the needle may strike the presser foot or needle plate and break. Also, turn corners gradually, in three to four small stitches.

FEET

The machine's "foot" is a foot-shaped metal or plastic piece that clips or screws on around the needle. The foot sits lightly on the fabric when set in the "down" position. For most sewing jobs, the standard *presser foot* keeps the fabric flat and close to the needle plate. This helps feed fabric into the underlying teeth which help move the material across the working surface.

Most machines come with several different feet, and additional feet for special purposes can be purchased separately. Feet are also often interchangeable among machine makes. Certain special feet are especially helpful in embroidery. The *embroidery foot,* often made of clear plastic with grooves on its "sole," glides smoothly over slight buildups of thread that will occur with satin stitch. The *darning foot* (which often doubles as an embroidery foot) allows free movement of cloth in *any* direction. There are special feet for hemming (so that a seam allowance is folded as you sew), buttonholes, zigzag, chain stitching, and zippers, among others.

Different feet are used to sew different fabrics and stitiches. From left to right: straight-stitch foot, overedge foot, zigzag foot, and special-purpose foot (hand-held).

10

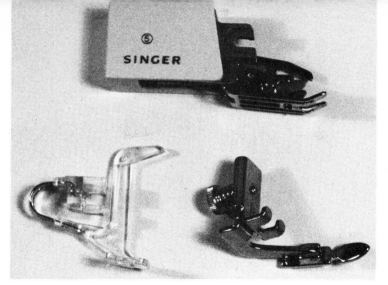

At the top, the Singer Even-Feed foot is shown. The Even-Feed foot improves the feeding of fabrics that tend to stick, stretch, or slip while being sewn by feeding both the top and bottom fabrics at the same time so that seams start even, feed evenly, and end even. At the bottom left, the darning or embroidery foot is shown. At the bottom right is the zipper foot.

A close-up of, from left to right: straight-stitch foot, overedge foot, zigzag foot, special-purpose foot.

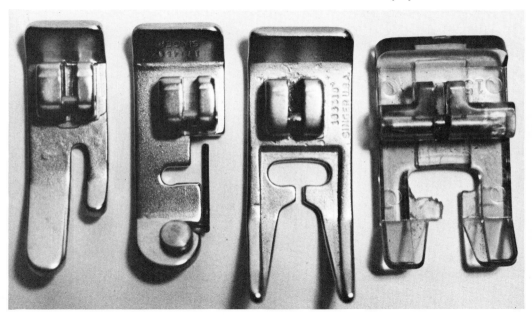

PLATES

Interchangeable metal plates are made to fit into the base of the sewing machine. The needle passes through the plate to reach the bobbin. Special plates may be required for certain special stitches, depending upon the machine. For example, special plates are often needed to make eyelets, or to sew circular designs.

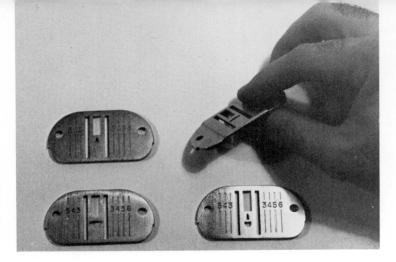

Different stitches may require the use of a special cover plate. At top left is the straight-stitch plate, at top right the zigzag plate for free embroidery, at bottom left a standard zigzag plate, and at bottom right the chain-stitch plate.

The teeth—"dog feet"—which guide fabric through the needle path protrude through the plate. It is necessary, when doing "free" machine embroidery, to lower or cover the teeth so that the fabric can be readily moved in any direction without resistance. Some machines are equipped with a mechanism to lower the teeth; others are equipped with plates that cover them.

BOBBINS

The bobbin is a small spool contained in the underside of the sewing machine, under the needle plate. It supplies the thread that interlocks with the upper threads to form a stitch. This mechanism will be discussed in Chapter 2. Many different kinds of thread can be wound onto bobbins either by your machine's usual method or by hand. Always keep extra bobbins on hand. The selection of a thread for the bobbin is yet another design consideration, since it may or may not be the same as the top thread that passes through the needle.

Most machines are set at the factory to release thread from the bobbin at a fixed tension. However, many bobbin cases have a small screw that can be turned to increase or decrease bobbin thread tension. Consult your instruction manual or machine representative if you have questions about making such adjustments. Being able to alter bobbin tension is still another element in your control of machine embroidery (and one separate from the ability to manipulate the tension

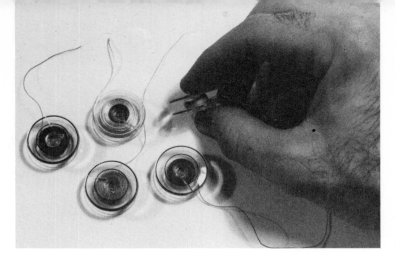

Clear plastic bobbins make it easy to see when bobbin thread is running low.

of the top thread). Note, however, that it is not possible to adjust the bobbin tension on all machines. If you intend to do a lot of machine embroidery involving altering bobbin tension, consider buying a second bobbin case. Allow one to remain at the tension set at the factory and vary the tension of the other.

THREADS

When equipping yourself to create machine embroidery, one of the best investments you can make is in a variety of threads. Threads vary not only in color, but in texture and composition (cotton, wool yarn, silk, and synthetics) as well. Experiment with threads of different types to determine how they behave under different adjustments, in combination with other threads, in

A wide variety of threads are made especially for or are suitable for machine embroidery. Threads may be of cotton, polyester, cotton-covered polyester, nylon, silk, and metallics. Leading manufacturers include Belding-Lily, J. P. Coats, Talon, and Rashtria-Aradhana.

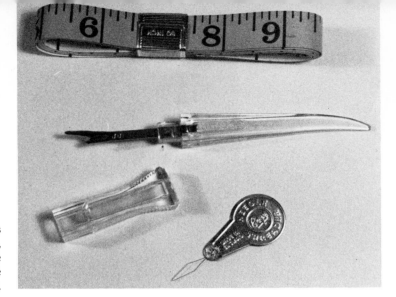

A wide range of sewing aids are available. A tape measure, seam ripper, and needle threader (top to bottom) are among the most useful.

combination with different fabrics, and in different stitches (straight, zigzag, automatic, and so forth).

Threads of all fibers can be used for machine embroidery, although the most commonly used threads are of polyester and of cotton, in size 50. Like every other variable in machine embroidery, thread should be considered a design element and, as such, a factor to be changed and experimented with to understand its potential. There are threads of invisible nylon, metallic threads, raffia threads, knitting yarn, silk embroidery thread, synthetic threads of acrylic and polyester. Even threads pulled out of fabrics can be used and often have exciting textures.

In evaluating threads, color is, of course, the most obvious quality, but many related factors should be considered. Does the color have the intensity you require? Is there a good range of colors in that line of thread? Is the texture right—is the thread too fine or plain, and is it likely to ravel, twist, or wiggle on the fabric or in the process of sewing? Is the thread glossy or matte? How will its reflectance interact with the fabric? Is the thread too difficult to work with? Is it strong enough to do the job, or is a heavier (lower number) thread needed? Look at how the thread behaves when used in different stitches: Does it stitch evenly? Is it better for bold straight stitching than for satin or pattern stitches?

With experimentation, one can learn quickly how different threads behave and what special effects they can produce. Don't forget that threads may look different on different fabrics.

When working with heavier threads, such as wool yarns, it may be necessary to work the "wrong side" of the fabric. Wrap these threads around the *bobbin,* because they will not readily pass through the machine and needle. If the bobbin thread is to appear on the face of the embroidery, the face of your work will be *facedown* during sewing. You will see the back of the piece as you work. This takes some getting used to, but can be quickly mastered.

A number of companies manufacture a wide variety of threads useful in machine embroidery. Belding-Lily, for example, makes the following threads, among others: quilting thread, Corticelli long-staple polyester, heavy-duty polyester, nylon, buttonhole twist (for-decorative top stitching), Corticelli pure silk twist, mercerized colorfast cotton, and Corticelli pure silk. J. P. Coats, in its Dual-Duty Plus line, makes cotton-covered polyester in standard weight as well as in an extrafine weight for machine embroidery and for lightweight fabrics. It makes an extrafine thread in variegated colors for shaded work. Talon offers metallic gold and silver threads as well as silk buttonhole-twist thread, and Rashtria-Aradhana markets an Indian silk thread for machine embroidery.

FABRICS

Embroidery can be executed on virtually any fabric that a needle can pass through—from light organza to vinyl, to hessian (burlap), to leather. Generally, firm, closely woven fabrics work best, and fabrics made of natural materials, such as cotton, usually pucker less than synthetics. Ultimately, however, the fabric chosen depends upon the surface effects one wants to create.

Janet Kuemmerlein uses textiles with contrasting textures and reflectance to create dramatic effects. In this piece (18" x 24"), silks and Mylar ® film were machine-sewn onto a background of black wool using a straight stitch. Beads were sewn on by hand. *Courtesy: Janet Kuemmerlein*

Here are a few tips on working with fabrics in machine embroidery:

• If it is intended that the final piece be washable, make certain the fabric has been preshrunk (by wetting the material lightly and drying). Be certain that both fabric and threads are colorfast. Beware of threads that will shrink or pull out during washing. Metallic threads, for example, do not tolerate washing.

• Embroider first, *then* cut out the final contours of the piece from the larger piece of fabric. Always arrange your design on the fabric so that there will be sufficient fabric border to accommodate seams.

• Reinforce flimsy fabrics by one of several methods to prevent puckering:

1. Baste a light fabric like organdy or organza to the back of the piece.
2. Iron on an interfacing such as Pellon®.
3. Apply spray starch to stiffen the fabric.
4. Embroider with typing paper between the fabric and needle plate. Pull away the paper after you've finished sewing.
5. Try decreasing the top thread tension—this will reduce most slight puckering.

• Always work out your stitches on scrap pieces of the same fabric before starting. In this way, you can

16

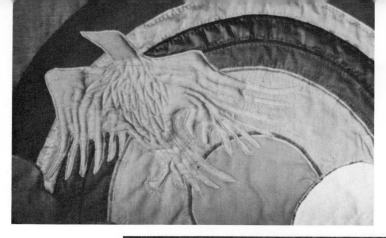

This detail of *Flight*, by Andrea Aldredge, shows its machine-appliquéd rainbow, hand-quilted sky, and machine-stitched trapunto bird. *Courtesy: Andrea Aldredge*

Shad, a collage of machine-embroidered appliqués machine-stitched to a machine-embroidered background. *Courtesy: Margaret Cusack*

A close-up of the zodiac portion of Sara Drower's *Fortune-Telling Dress* shows her detailed painting, machine embroidery, and light quilting. *Photos courtesy Sara Drower*

Sara Drower's *Fortune-Telling Dress* of hand-painted fabric was lightly machine-quilted and the outlines of the zodiac and clouds were machine-embroidered.

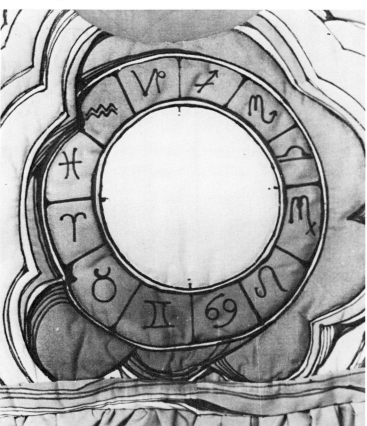

A machine-quilted box (8″ each side) by Josephine Schwartz. *Courtesy: Josephine Schwartz*

Aqueous Ecstasy (30″ x 24″), machine-sewn satin stuffed in the trapunto technique by Sandra Ward. *Courtesy: Sandra Ward*

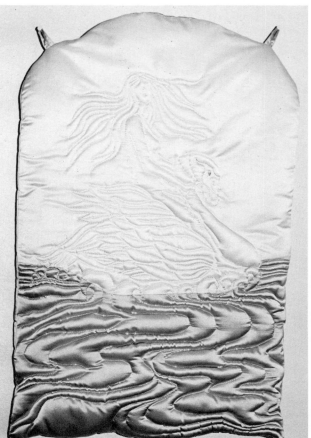

18

Every Cloud Has a Secret Zip-In Lining (24″ x 80″), hand-painted silk satin machine-quilted and -embroidered, by Sara Drower. *Courtesy: Sara Drower*

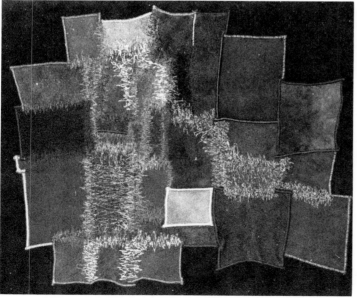

Animal Fiber VI (18″ x 16″), a wall piece in suede machine-embroidered and -appliquéd with silk thread, by Anna V. A. Polesný. *Courtesy: Anna V. A. Polesný*

determine the most appropriate stitch lengths, widths, and tensions. You will also get a feel for the speed at which to work and how to handle the material and thread without making errors on the fabric that will be used in the finished piece.

Remember that the characteristics of the fabric are important to consider in designing any embroidery. Pretty stitchery can be lost in a deep-pile velvet. Heavy twill can distort embroidered lines in ways that may or may not be desired. In short, every fabric has idiosyncracies to be exploited by clever design, but must in any event be taken into account. Fabrics should be thought of in terms of their color, reflectance, texture, and practicality. Whether they are woven or knit, printed or plain, most fabrics have an intrinsic pattern. Fabrics with slubbed threads, or those with loose weaves and textures such as burlaps, often will not accommodate machine embroidery. Heavy fabrics may call for bolder patterns of stitchery. Complex embroidery may be inappropriate on a highly textured tweed. A glossy silk ground may overwhelm stitchery in a matte cotton thread. There are no rules. The key to success is experimentation with fabric and with thread. Where possible, experiment with scraps until you achieve the desired effect. Keep a record of successful combinations of fabric, thread, stitch, and machine settings.

The qualities and uses of different fabrics will be discussed further in Chapter 3 and throughout the book.

OTHER SUPPLIES

In addition to the materials and supplies mentioned above, you will find certain other items extremely helpful to have on hand. They include:

• Medium-size *scissors* for cutting fabric and snipping threads are a must. Scissors for cutting paper, and *pinking shears,* for cutting fabric edges, would also be useful.

Machine-embroidered collar on a batik gown.

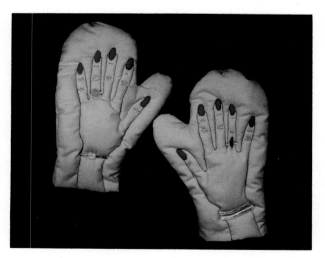

Quilted oven mitts by Thelma R. Newman.

A corded Ultrasuede ® pillow by Thelma R. Newman.

Cityscape at Night, wall hanging in appliqué by Margaret Cusack. *Courtesy: Margaret Cusack*

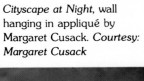

Ultrasuede® patchwork skirt by Thelma R. Newman.

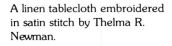

A linen tablecloth embroidered in satin stitch by Thelma R. Newman.

"Animal Fibre VI" (18" x 16"), a small wall
piece of suede appliquéd and embroidered
with silk thread, by Anna V. A. Polesný.
Courtesy Anna V. A. Polesný

Big-apple bag in embroidered felt by Thelma
R. Newman.

Nude Act pillows (each 14" x 17") by Margaret Cusack. *Courtesy: Margaret Cusack*

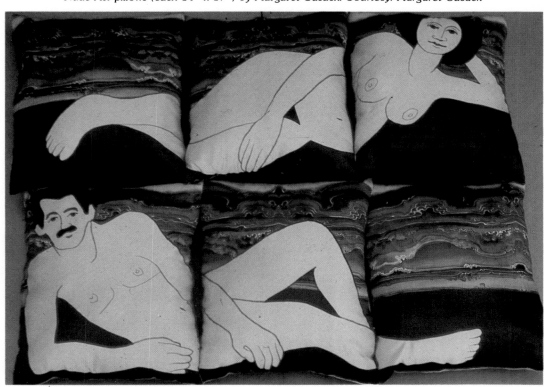

Appliqué wall hanging by Jane Bearman.

Clown bags of machine-appliquéd and
-embroidered suede by Anna V. A. Polesný.
Courtesy: Anna V. A. Polesný

A close-up of *Animal Fiber V,*
straight-stitched suede, a wall
piece by Anna V. A. Polesný.
Courtesy: Anna V. A. Polesný

"Animal Fibre XIV" (26" x 60"), machine-embroidered suede with machine lacework by Anna V. A. Polesný. *Courtesy Anna V. A. Polesný*

A machine-embroidered pendant by Joan Schulze. *Courtesy: Joan Schulze*

Machine-embroidered fabric appliquéd to terry cloth towels.

Close-up of flowers and leaves of couched silk cord on a wool skirt by Thelma R. Newman.

Kew Gardens (16″ x 14″), machine embroidery and appliqué by Joan Schulze. *Courtesy: Joan Schulze*

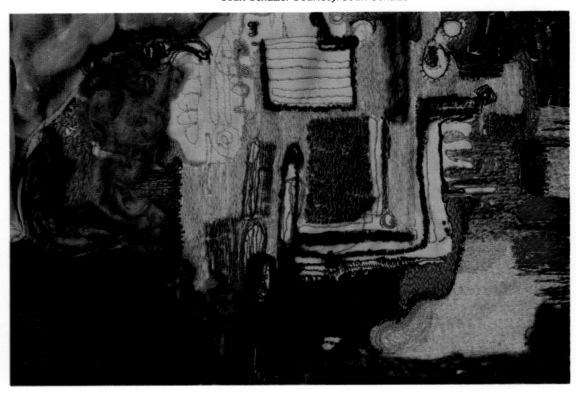

Close Encounters, machine-appliquéd and stuffed suede and leather by Doreen Lah. *Courtesy: Doreen Lah*

Lower portion of machine-embroidered linen skirt by Thelma R. Newman.

Machine-embroidered pocket appliquéd to machine-embroidered sundress by Thelma R. Newman.

A close-up of *Mysterie,*
machine appliqué embroidery
by Doreen Lah. *Courtesy:*
Doreen Lah

Rainbow Wonder #2, a dress
of hand-painted fabric
machine-embroidered and
quilted by Sara Drower.
Courtesy: Sara Drower

Machine-embroidered and appliquéd skirt by Thelma
R. Newman.

Sleeping bag in trapunto, quilting, and embroidery by Elizabeth S. Gurner. *Courtesy: Elizabeth S. Gurrier*

Barbara Lambert's machine-
and hand-sewn muslin stuffed
sculptures dispense tissues
from a box hidden within.
Courtesy: Barbara F. Lambert

• A *seam ripper* will be indispensable, especially when you've decided to remove entire rows of satin stitching.

• A *tape measure* and a *ruler* are essential when precision is desired.

• A *needle threader* is particularly helpful with difficult, thick threads.

• *Tailor's chalk* and a *marking pen* are essential tools for design.

• *Embroidery hoops* (six to eight inches in diameter) keep free embroidery taut in the absence of a presser foot (see Chapter 2).

• *Graph paper, tissue paper, construction paper, and typing paper* are useful in creating designs to be translated to fabric, actually transferring designs to the fabric, and reinforcing flimsy fabrics for embroidery.

• *Straight pins* are valuable sewing aids, particularly when sewing appliqué.

Machine-appliquéd and
-embroidered pillows by
Margaret Cusack. *Courtesy:
Margaret Cusack*

Stripes and Heart (70" x 32"), a wall quilt in red, brick green, and magenta by Lenore Davis. The fabric, a cotton velveteen, was painted with textile dye. The painted fabric was then machine-quilted over a layer of polyester batting with a muslin backing. The half circles and heart were stuffed with extra polyester filling by slitting the muslin backing, inserting stuffing, and closing the backing with hand stitching. A final lining was basted to the back of the piece and the whole was edged with cotton velveteen to create a ½" border. *Courtesy: Lenore Davis*

• An *ironing board* and *iron* need no explanation. Steam is the best weapon against minor puckering.

• *Fabric adhesives,* including all-purpose white glue and adhesives made especially for sewing purposes come in handy when there are many threads to be tied off behind the piece—a small daub of glue can save time and energy that would otherwise be spent tying.

In this chapter we have considered general equipment of machine embroidery. In Chapter 2 we will explore basic principles: how the sewing machine works, how to develop a vocabulary of embroidery stitches, and how to create a design and transfer it to fabric.

Quilt designed by Charles Counts and executed by the Rising Fawn Quilters. *Courtesy: Rising Fawn Quilters*

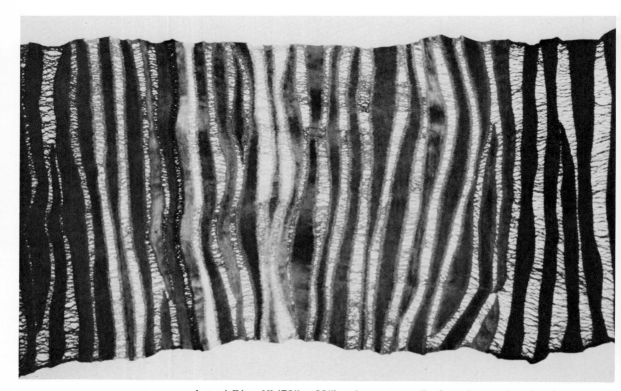

Animal Fiber XI (70" x 39"), a hanging scroll of machine-embroidered suede joined with machine lace of silk thread, by Anna V. A. Polesný. *Courtesy: Anna V. A. Polesný*

2

MACHINE EMBROIDERY

This chapter focuses on the creation of machine embroidery, including the way the sewing machine works, the variety of stitches, and the ways in which stitches are combined to create unique designs. Bear in mind that this chapter should be no more than a beginning—the best way to develop the skills to make machine embroidery is to experiment with different materials and threads and to conduct your own investigations into the possible combinations of stitches.

A richly machine-embroidered pendant by Joan Schulze. *Courtesy: Joan Schulze*

25

HOW THE SEWING MACHINE WORKS

If you understand how the sewing machine forms a stitch, you place this tool under your complete command. It need not be a mysterious box that somehow "sews." If you learn how your machine works and become a good troubleshooter, you will feel much less frustrated with its behavior and feel more comfortable about experimenting with it.

Sewing machines form stitches by causing two threads to interlock with the fabric between them. Simply stated, when the needle passes through the fabric, it carries the top thread down with it. A small loop of thread forms on the underside of the cloth when the needle passes through it. This loop is caught by a small hooklike projection from the edge of the bobbin case that enters the loop, enlarges it, and then rotates in one full circle to pull the loop of top thread over and around the entire bobbin. In so doing, the hook in effect pulls the top thread around the bottom thread that is being released from the bobbin. As the needle is pulled up through the fabric, the tension on the top thread is increased. The thread slides off the bobbin hook and pulls up a small loop of bobbin thread with which it has become intertwined through the fabric. Feed dogs then move the fabric a fraction of an inch, and the next stitch is begun as the needle moves down through the fabric.

At the normal tension setting, the top and bottom threads interlock midway through the fabric, giving the "dotted line" appearance of normal machine stitching. Different effects can be achieved by adjusting the tension of the thread. If the top tension is increased (by adjusting the tension setting on the machine) the top thread will pull bobbin thread more, bringing the bottom thread closer to the top surface of the fabric. This gives the appearance of a straight line of top thread lying on the surface of the fabric. This effect is called the "whipstitch" or "beading."

Conversely, if the top tension is reduced, or if the tension of the bobbin thread is increased (bobbin thread tension cannot be adjusted on all machines), the top thread will be pulled down through the fabric toward the underside. This is called a "cable stitch." Low top-tension settings are usually employed when one wants to work a design and sew on the "wrong side" of the fabric (the "right" side facedown on the machine). It is often necessary to work with the front of the fabric facedown on the machine when you want to embroider with or apply heavy yarns, slubbed threads, or other threads that cannot be threaded through the needle. Such threads usually can be hand-wound onto the bobbin and "whipstitched" upside down to what will become the face of the work.

With an understanding of how stitches are formed, one can begin to understand how mistakes are made. For example, why is a stitch skipped when fabric is not held flat? The needle passes through the fabric and the top thread forms a loop—but because the fabric has been raised above the needle plate, the loop is also raised and the bobbin hook misses it. Whenever the loop is not hooked by the bobbin hook, a stitch is dropped. See the chart on *Troubleshooting* (p. 28) for solutions to some commonly encountered problems.

PREPARING THE MACHINE FOR EMBROIDERY

There are two basic ways of using the sewing machine to create embroidery. If the machine is set for normal straight stitching (the feed dogs are in place and the pressure foot is in the down position) the machine will pull the fabric through, and gentle curves and turns can be executed.

The alternative machine embroidery technique is known as "free movement embroidery" or "free embroidery." It is a much more flexible and exciting technique and allows a much fuller use of the machine. In free embroidery, fabric can be moved in *any* direction as you sew, permitting you to execute intricate designs, create free-form stitchery, and manipulate stitch direc-

TROUBLESHOOTING

Problem	Possible reasons
Upper thread frequently breaks	—Presser foot may not be down —Machine might be threaded incorrectly —Needle might be inserted backward —Needle may be blunt or bent —Upper tension may be too tight —Needle aperture might be too small for the thickness of thread, causing the thread to fray and break —You might be trying to sew through too thick a layer of fabric, causing thread to fray and break —Moving the fabric too quickly can snap the thread —Old thread may be dried out and brittle (moisture can sometimes be restored by keeping a thread in the refrigerator for a while)
Lower (bobbin) thread breaks	—Bobbin tension might be too tight, if the machine has this adjustment —Thread may not be evenly wound on bobbin
Stitch fails to form	—Needle might be threaded from the wrong side —Needle might be inserted backward —Needle might be inserted too far up —Fabric might not be held flat against needle plate —Needle may be bent —If all else fails, machine's timing may be off; check with manufacturer's representative
Needle breaks	—Needle may be inserted incorrectly —Wrong needle plate or wrong foot may be used (e.g., wide zigzagging cannot be done through the narrow hole found in the straight-stitch needle plate). If the needle strikes the plate or foot, it will snap off —Upper thread tension may be too tight —Fabric may be being jerked too quickly while needle is in motion, causing the needle to bend or hit the foot or needle plate

28

Fabric puckers	—Top tension or bottom tension may be too tight
	—Stitches may be too long; decrease stitch length
	—Thread may be too heavy for fabric
	—Fabric may need extra body—e.g., fusible backings, spray starch, organdy backing, typing-paper backing
	—Fabric may have been jerked away from machine, causing fabric to gather
	—Especially in free-motion embroidery, the apposition of various stitches will cause puckering; this can be used as a special effect in the piece, or can often be eliminated with steam ironing

tion and length by controlling the movement of the fabric. Free embroidery is usually worked in an embroidery hoop six to eight inches in diameter. The hoop keeps the fabric flat and allows you to control the movement of the fabric by controlling the movement of the hoop. To prepare your machine for free embroidery:

1. Lower the feed dogs (some machines have a dial for lowering them below the working surface of the machine) or cover them with the special plate provided with the machine. In this way nothing will force the fabric to move in any particular direction.

2. Remove the standard pressure foot, and substitute an all-purpose foot, an embroidery foot, or a darning foot. Such feet come with most machines and can also be purchased separately. Often they are made of clear plastic to enable you to see each stitch as it is formed.

3. Decrease the pressure of the foot. Many machines can be adjusted for a "darning" or "embroidery" pressure, in which the foot rests more lightly on the surface of the fabric and therefore will not cause the fabric to bind even when embroidered stitches build up.

4. Set stitch length selector to zero so that the length of the stitch will depend solely upon movement of the fabric.

5. Set thread tension a little lower than normal. Bobbin tension usually will not require adjustment, except for special effects, but, if possible, bypass the bobbin tension, too.

6. Set the pattern selector for the stitch you want to use—straight, zigzag, feather, and so on.

7. Set the stitch-width selector to desired width.

8. Set the sewing speed to the "slow" position. You will want to aim for a speed that allows you to work smoothly, without jerking the hoop. Some machines, such as the Singer Touch-Tronic, are equipped to do a "hesitation stitch"—a speed basting stitch with an extra time lapse between needle penetrations to allow you to move the hoop less hurriedly.

9. Stretch the fabric in an embroidery hoop, and make certain that the fabric is very *taut*. If the fabric flutters, you may drop stitches. To keep the fabric taut, wrap the hoops with strips of cotton or bias binding tape. Hoops are available in wood or plastic. Some are designed especially for use in machine embroidery so that they easily pass under the needle. Any fabric can be used in free-movement embroidery, but tight weaves tend to be more difficult to handle.

10. Read the machine manual to be certain you have prepared the machine properly for free movement.

To begin, slide the hooped fabric under the needle so that the fabric lies flat on the machine surface. Lower the presser bar. Note that even though you are not using the presser foot, the bar must be in the *down position* in order to engage the upper thread tension. Lock the initial stitch, bring both threads to the surface and cut extra thread.

Keep your index and third fingers moving alongside the needle to make certain the fabric stays flat, and use your thumbs to guide the hoop, but be careful not to place your fingers too close to the sharp needle.

In time you may decide to abandon use of the hoop, and to keep the fabric taut under the needle using only your fingers. But, in the beginning, use the frame.

Try to remain relaxed while embroidering, and feed the fabric through the needle at an even pace. When you first begin, stitches may pile up on one another because you are not moving the fabric fast enough. You may find that stitches are too far apart because you have moved the fabric too quickly. Achieving the correct speed takes practice.

To begin, practice embroidering on a medium-weight cotton fabric with cotton sewing thread. Wind a different color thread in the bobbin so you can see what happens to the bobbin thread when the tension is varied. Vary the tension of the thread frequently to determine what different effects are possible—thread tension can have a greater impact upon the result than you might think. To test yourself and to develop your skill, draw a few shapes—circles, spirals, squares—on the cloth with tailor's chalk and attempt to embroider those practice patterns at a smooth, steady pace.

DEVELOPING A STITCH VOCABULARY

The majority of this chapter's photographs and captions are concerned with the development of a vocabulary of machine embroidery stitches through experimentation. Each basic type of stitch lends itself to particular uses, and each can be altered to produce special, unusual effects. Learning how to generate and control special effects is like learning the different ways of applying paint to a canvas.

The *straight stitch* is surprisingly versatile. It is useful for outlining, as, for example, in the trapunto discussed in Chapter 4. It can be used to secure a design or a piece of fabric to a background, as in appliqué. Straight stitching with thick threads can be used to add emphasis, too. Like any stitch, straight stitching can be continuous or broken, used in a single line or repeated. Lines of straight stitching may be crosshatched to fill space or to create texture. Try decorating a piece of cloth with a design in cross-hatching and using this "new" fabric as an element of appliqué on another piece of cloth. As mentioned above, the many variations on straight stitch include the whipstitch (produced by increasing the tension of the top thread) and the cable stitch (produced by reducing the tension on the top thread or increasing the tension on the bobbin thread).

Developing a Vocabulary of Machine Stitches

Straight Stitch

Even the basic straight stitch need not be dull. This straight-stitch outline, transferred from a photograph to tracing paper to fabric, is simple but strong.

The following sequence of photographs illustrates how straight and zigzag stitches may be combined and how designs may be developed using simple elemental stitches. By mastering the "vocabulary" of basic machine stitches illustrated in this chapter, you will soon be able to express your ideas for machine embroidery quickly and fluently.

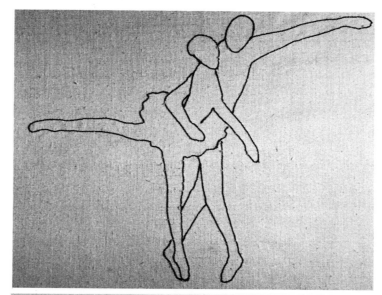

The straight stitch was used to sew the general outline of a carafe. Without modeling the shapes, however, no one would know that the outline was intended to define a three-dimensional form. The outline was modeled by using parallel horizontal straight stitches. With the addition of those rows of stitching, the formerly flat outline appears to take shape. The length and spacing create the illusion of light and shadow.

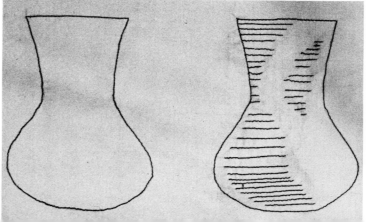

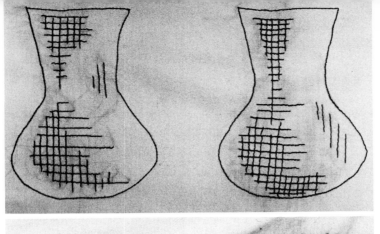

The same effect can be achieved by combining vertical and horizontal lines. This "cross-hatching" is similar to the technique used by artists and cartoonists. Different intensities of light and dark space can be created by varying the density of the cross-hatching. Different effects can also be achieved by closely stitching the horizontal rows and widely spacing the vertical rows, or vice versa.

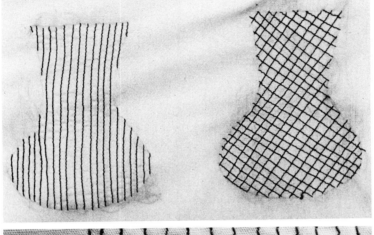

Forms also may be defined in exciting ways without attempting to create the illusion of three-dimensionality. In these examples, straight stitches were used to create shapes with distinct patterns and textures—without outlining.

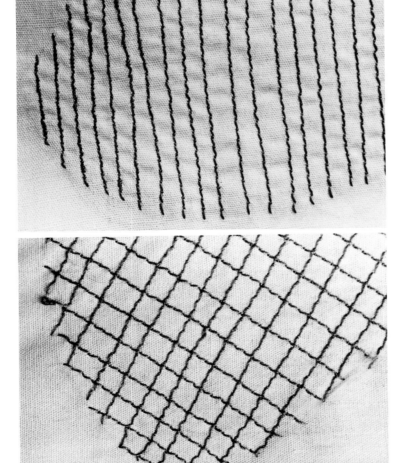

The *zigzag* is the standby favorite of most machine embroiderers because by changing its width and length a wide range of different effects can be achieved. Many short adjacent zigzag stitches form the *satin stitch:* it has a rich, thick quality. The satin stitch is so handsome and versatile that we urge you to practice perfecting it. Find the thread tension, width, length, and speed settings that produce the best result and write those settings down. You will want to be able to return to this old friend. Satin stitch looks smoothest when it is done at high speed. Use an embroidery foot and a lower than normal top-thread tension. Extra-fine thread will improve the quality of the stitch, and because it is a heavy stitch—involving a lot of thread—use it on fabrics with sufficient body, or support the fabric. Flimsy fabric may be backed with typing paper or organdy, or stiffened with spray starch. Such reinforcement will prevent the satin stitch from causing the fabric to pucker too much. To avoid the buildup of an excessive thickness of thread at turned corners, use the following method to make a sharp turn: stop the stitching when the needle is through the fabric, on the outer edge, raise the presser bar, turn the fabric (pivoting on the needle), lower the presser bar and resume sewing. As to variations, the same kind of "beading" effect produced in straight stitch by increasing top-thread tension can be produced with satin stitch. For a special effect, try using a different color bobbin thread when sewing a beaded satin stitch. (Note that the stitch can misbehave if you stop the machine in the middle of a row of stitches.)

Zigzag Stitch

The zigzag stitch is frequently used as a border for designs, as a means of attaching pieces of cloth to other fabrics in appliqué, and as the elemental component of the "satin stitch." The satin stitch is no more than short zigzag stitches formed one next to the other to achieve the effect of a wide unbroken line of smooth, slightly raised thread on the fabric. Here a satin stitch is used to outline the shape of a carafe. At left, the same width of satin stitch was used throughout. At right, the width of the stitch was varied to create a more visually exciting design.

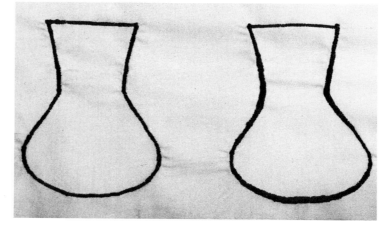

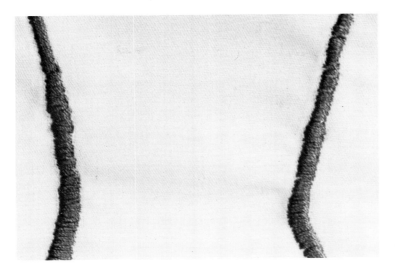

A close-up of the satin stitch used on the carafes.

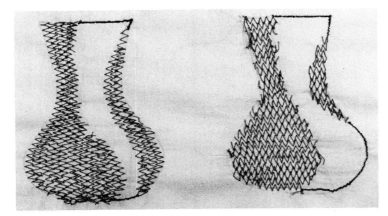

Widely spaced zigzag stitches— horizontal and vertical. Note that variety stitches, such as the zigzag stitch, may take the place of outlining in the straight stitch or may be used in combination with it.

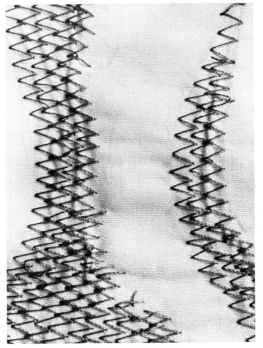

Vertical zigzag stitching can assume many rhythms depending on how it is placed and spaced.

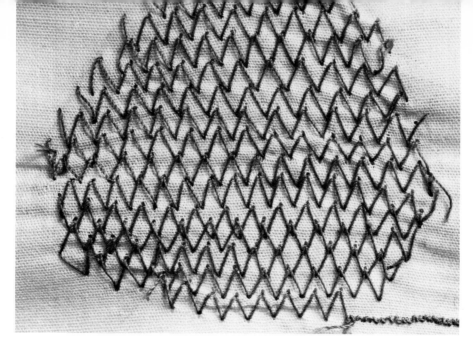

Horizontal zigzag stitching
seems to undulate.

A variety of rich surface
textures can be produced using
different densities of zigzag
stitching in random directions.
In the design on the right, the
entire area was filled with
random zigzag and no fabric
was allowed to remain visible.
These pieces were executed
using the "hesitation stitch"
option on the Touch-Tronic
2000, in which the needle
pauses for a moment out of
the fabric, to allow a little more
time to decide where to put the
next stitch. This is "free-motion
embroidery," done without a
presser foot, in an embroidery
hoop. When you are dealing
with large buildups of thread, it
is usually necessary to work on
heavier material to avoid
puckering, or else to back the
material with interfacing or
organza.

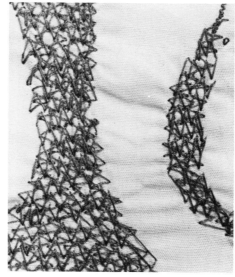

A close-up showing the texture
of random open zigzag stitches.

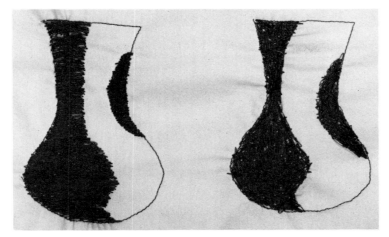

Free-motion embroidery can look orderly or rough in texture, depending on how one turns the fabric. On the left, the fabric was stitched with a long zigzag stitch in the horizontal only. At right, stitching direction was purposefully random.

A close-up showing free embroidery using long horizontal zigzag stitches.

Another close-up showing the use of shorter horizontal zigzag stitches.

37

Random long zigzag stitches. When you are doing free embroidery, either work without the presser foot or use a special embroidery foot. When no presser foot is used, be careful to keep the fabric taut and flat, using your fingers. Some machines, like the Singer Touch-Tronic 2000, allow the pressure that the foot applies to the cloth to be adjusted. When you are doing free embroidery with a foot in place, the pressure of the foot should be as light as possible.

A rich, active texture may be produced using the darning stitch. A darning foot was set to low pressure and the fabric was worked in the horizontal direction only.

A close-up of the darning stitch shows its loopy, almost furry texture.

Many of the newer machines, particularly those by Singer, offer a varity of *automatic stitches* which greatly extend the range of decorative possibilities. Electric machines such as the Singer Touch-Tronic adjust to these special stitches automatically, making it easy to explore their uses. Doodling on a piece of fabric is especially important to determine whether the fabric is suitable and to determine the proper character of the stitch. If stitches cause the fabric to pucker, reinforce the material. Also note that automatic stitches, because they often repeat a design, pose problems in turning corners. It may be necessary to measure the length of each stitch to determine how many can fit within a given space. Always try to turn corners at the completion of a

Automatic Stitches

The newest generation of electronic sewing machines is simple to use and very versatile. They also offer a wide variety of "automatic stitches" in which the sewing machine follows a complete, complex stitch pattern. The following series of stitches were made by the Touch-Tronic 2000. *From Left to Right:* (a) double needle scallop stitch, (b) stretch stitch, (c) ribbon stitch, (d) zigzag point stitch, (e) zigzag, (f) ricrac stitch, (g) leaf stitch, (h) honeycomb, (i) alternating bead stitch and arrowhead stitch, (j) Paris point stitch, (k) featherstitch, (l) overedge stretch stitch, (m) dog stitch, (n) icicle stitch, (o) Greek key stitch, (p) double-needle straight stitch. *Courtesy: The Singer Company*

stitch program. Another way of handling squared corners with automatic stitches is to embroider the pattern on a band of material, cut the band at a 45-degree angle and seam the edge. The cut and seamed band may then be appliquéd to the squared corner of the fabric to be decorated using zigzag or another decorative stitch.

For decorative borders and trims, also try combinations of special stitches. Combine them to create rows. Reverse the direction of sewing to get a mirror-image effect. Overlap different programmed stitches to create new stitch patterns. Let your imagination and experiments guide you to the development of a larger and more active vocabulary.

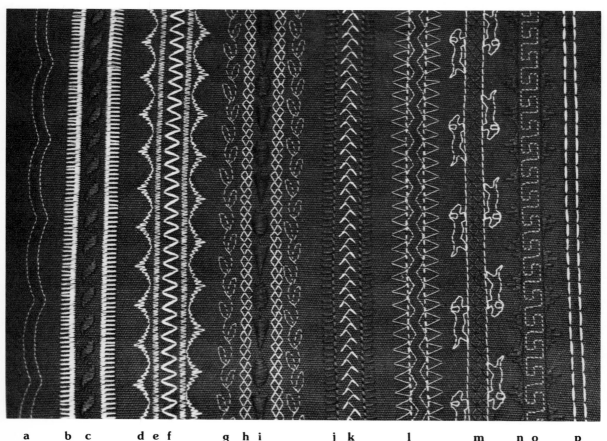

a   b   c   d e f   g h i   j k   l   m   n o   p

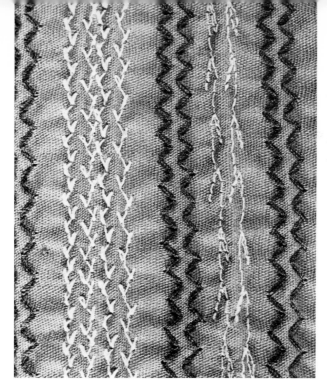

This close-up shows an active featherstitch, the ricrac stitch (like a double zigzag, and, therefore, bolder than plain zigzag), and a leaf stitch.

This set of stitches was a practice exercise to determine how different stitch patterns would work on net fabric. At bottom, each stitch was sewn at a slow speed, progressing to fast feed at the top. This illustrates how the stitches can be manipulated by varying the rate at which the work is passed through the machine. Intricate stitches that require the machine to sew forward and backward (e.g., surf stitch, tulip stitch) lose their pattern entirely when the fabric is pulled through the machine too rapidly. By knowing how each stitch is affected by speed of sewing, stitch length, and stitch width, you can avoid mistakes and take advantage of stitch distortions.

The special stitches shown here include the (a) Greek key stitch, (b) double-needle straight stitch, (c) surf stitch, (d) bead stitch, and (e) straight stitch.

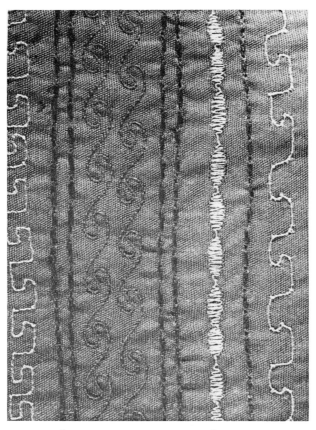

a   b   c   d e

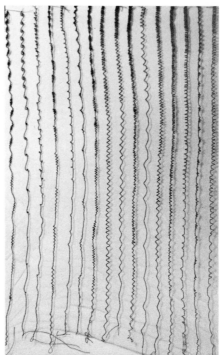

To sew on net fabrics, the pressure of the presser foot should be as low as possible (darning position), and the fabric should be guided carefully through the machine with both hands, holding the net taut. At the left side of the sampler, fabric was fed very slowly. At right, the fabric was fed very quickly. The stitches, from top to bottom, are:

1. Zigzag: produces a very loose stitch at high rate of feed;
2. Overedge stretch stitch: this stitch works well even at higher speeds;
3. Icicle stitch: faster feeding spreads out the design. You can speed the feed between stitching peaks to get more space between stitches and even produce a very pleasant seemingly wiggly stitch, as at far right;
4. Paris point stitch: as with the zigzag, when you feed the fabric through quickly the stitch becomes quite loose;
5. Elastic stretch stitch: design is, again, distorted and lost when you sew quickly or too slowly;
6. Featherstitch: design is lost if the fabric is pulled through the machine too quickly. A moderate speed must be maintained to produce the programmed pattern;
7. Scallop stitch: the frequency and depth of the arc described by the stitch are directly related to the speed of feed. Slow feeding produces a tight scallop, fast creates a lazy wavy line;
8. Ricrac stitch: slow sewing gives a bold three-dimensional line;

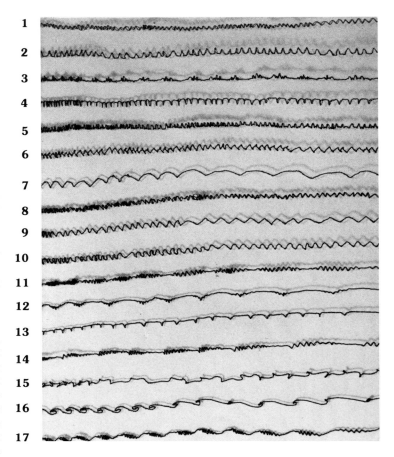

1
2
3
4
5
6
7
8
9
10
11
12
13
14
15
16
17

DESIGN AND DESIGN TRANSFER

Ideas for embroidery can come from almost anywhere—original ideas out of the blue, magazine photos, natural forms. No matter what the source of your inspiration, if you can cut the design out of paper, it certainly can be translated to fabric. Paper has the advantage of allowing you to try out different colors before making a final commitment to fabric. Try cutting out a unit and repeating it in various ways. Look for contrasting lights and darks.

Everyone can create good original design. Have faith in your imagination. New ideas will come to you if you open up to the world about you in a new way.

42

Focus close up by looking at the details of something, or look more expansively by eliminating details from your vision and selectively searching for major patterns. For example, direct your vision close up looking at a feather, perhaps a peacock feather. Note the pattern and repeat shapes within the form. Or broadly scrutinize the fenestration of a building. What kind of pattern and arrangement are made by the windows? Toys, birds, cacti, bottles, brain corals, sunflowers, a tree trunk, a group of mushrooms, are a few rich sources of inspiration.

Be even more courageous and take a journey into your dream world. What kind of whimsical fantasy forms will grow there? Collect ideas as you leaf through a magazine and store them for future reference.

The best ideas come from *simple* forms, abstractions from nature, or geometric shapes. The best design is one that is direct, honest, clear, essential. Don't *try* to be elegant, original, or different; what usually comes out is less than a clear, honest, and essential result. Don't try to realistically match the red skin of an apple with a red fabric. Try black or brown, for example. Stitchery today is often marked by slavish imitation of old patterns. These pieces lack that spontaneity or dynamism found in an improvisation or an original piece. About all one can say for these imitations is that they took a lot of work and skill to make. What a pity!

The trick to embroidering any design is finding a way of transferring the idea to fabric. Don't try to transfer *every* line of a design onto the fabric. Just transfer the main outlines of the design. Make a kind of cartoon of the design. Once the basic outline has been transferred onto the fabric it is easy to fill in the details as you embroider.

Often the cartoon is not the same size as what you want to embroider. Perhaps the easiest way to increase or reduce the scale of a drawing is to transfer the drawing to graph paper. Then, by using larger or smaller grids, you can scale up or scale down. The grid makes it easy to recopy the pattern, one square at a time.

9. Multistitch zigzag: if pulled through quickly, an effect similar to that produced with a scallop stitch may be achieved;
10. Honeycomb stitch: this stitch bears no resemblance to the programmed design when the rate of feed is increased;
11. Bead stitch;
12. Zigzag point stitch: like the other complex stitches, the design is distorted when fabric is pulled through the machine at high speed;
13. Blindstitch;
14. Arrowhead stitch: when the fabric is pulled through the machine quickly the arrowhead spreads out; it begins to look somewhat like the bead stitch;
15. Leaf stitch: the leaf stitch loses most of its form if pulled through the machine quickly, but if the presser foot pressure is increased, some of the complexity of the stitch can be restored, even on net;
16. Surf stitch: with presser foot at normal pressure, the wave behaves well until fast feeding begins to pull it apart;
17. Ribbon stitch: presser foot pressure should be set at normal for this stitch too.

There are many ways to transfer designs from paper to paper or from paper to fabric:

• You can always *work directly,* drawing outlines of shapes directly onto the fabric using a light pencil line. Tailor's chalk and dressmaker's pencil also are well suited to this purpose. Some pencil lines will be indelible, so beware—make certain that the embroidery will cover all lines. If the final piece is to be washable, use a waterproof pencil or ink to avoid a smeared catastrophe.

• *Cut paper shapes* may serve as templates. Trace around these with pencil or chalk, right onto the fabric.

• Trace the design onto *tracing paper.* With most fabrics you can lay the cloth over the paper, hold the two up to a window, and retrace the design onto the fabric. The backlighting helps make the design visible through the fabric.

• Since a piece of sheer *organza* is frequently used to back fabrics in machine embroidery, you can use this as the vehicle for transferring designs. Trace the design onto translucent organza. Baste the organza onto the wrong side of the fabric. Baste the outline of the design onto the organza/fabric combination.

• Trace or draw the design onto *iron-on interfacing.* Iron the interfacing onto the back of the fabric. Baste the design outline through the interfacing/fabric combination. This method produces a mirror image of the original design.

• Trace with an empty ball-point pen on *dressmaker's carbon paper.* Push firmly but do not tear the paper. Be careful—it has a tendency to smudge, but is extremely useful.

• *"Prick and pounce"* is a traditional transfer technique. Puncture tiny holes in the tracing paper cartoon, using a needle. (You can even "sew" a pierced dotted line on an empty sewing machine.) Place the pricked paper over the fabric. Special pounce powder—a kind of chalk powder—is rubbed over the holes. A dotted chalk line will result where the chalk has passed through the holes in the paper out onto the fabric. This technique works less well on heavy fabrics because the dots tend to disappear or rub out. This technique is especially good for repeat patterns, because the same piece of pricked paper can be moved to another spot and "pounced" again and again.

• Special *transfer pens* (e.g., Pressure-Fax® by Graphic Techniques Co.) are an excellent way to transfer designs. Trace the design onto tissue paper with felt-tip pen. Flip the paper over and retrace it with the transfer pen. Lay the paper on the fabric with the transfer ink side down. Pin the paper to the fabric. Iron it to transfer the ink on the back of the cartoon to the face of the fabric.

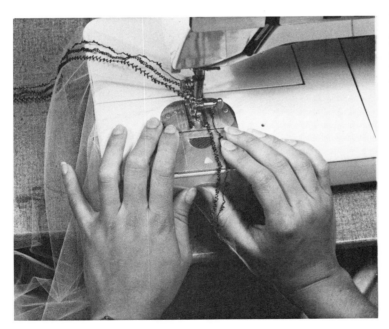

Net Scarf

Net fabrics should be held very flat and taut if an embroidery hoop is not used. Because netting is often very fine, it may not feed through the machine automatically but may need to be pushed and pulled through at an even pace.

45

The stitches used to embroider this border were *(left to right):*
1. Paris point stitch: moving slowly, presser foot pressure set to lowest position;
2. Zigzag stitch: same settings;
3. Featherstitch: slow pace, presser foot pressure at normal fabric setting;
4. Ribbon stitch: moderate speed, presser foot pressure normal;
5. Honeycomb stitch: slow pace, presser foot pressure normal;
6. Surf Stitch: slow pace, presser foot pressure normal;
7. Leaf stitch: slow pace, presser foot pressure normal.

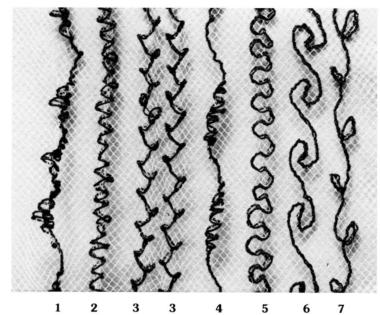

1   2   3   3   4   5   6   7

Black polyester thread was used to produce a dramatic but delicate border on this net scarf.

46

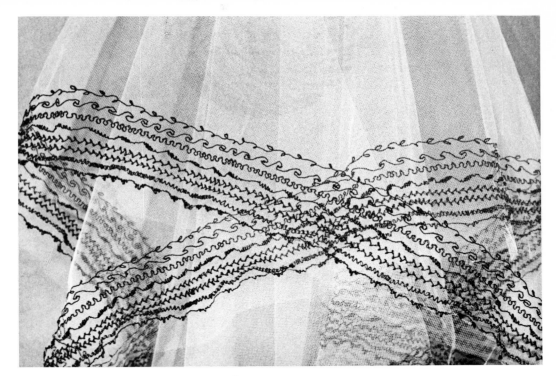

Close-up view of the border on the net scarf.

Machine-Embroidered Pillow Cases

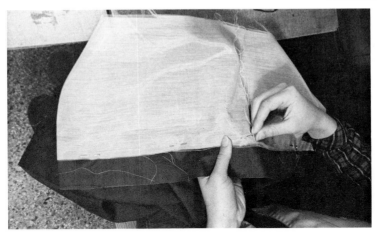

Rows of different stitches can make a pretty border design. Here, a plain weave pillow case is to be embroidered. The hem is opened in order to allow a piece of an interfacing material to be pinned in place and hand-basted to the inside of the pillow case. This interfacing provides a basis for the embroidery and thereby minimizes puckering that might otherwise be caused by embroidering on such thin cloth.

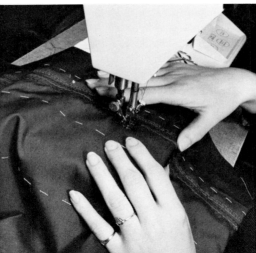

The pillow case is basted in white thread parallel to its ends as a guide in embroidering. Tailor's chalk or another marking system could also have been used. The clear plastic presser foot was used so that the stitches could be seen as they were being formed.

47

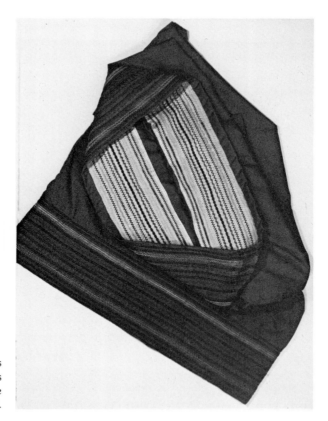

When the embroidery was finished, excess interfacing was trimmed and the edge of the pillow case was re-hemmed.

Another set of pillow cases was embroidered using twin needles. Twin needles produce twin rows of stitches in the same or different colors of thread. They speed the creation of an embroidered border. Here, ricrac stitch, featherstitch, leaf stitch, ribbon stitch, and bead stitch were used.

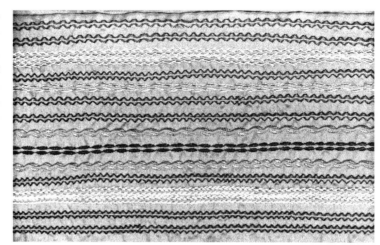

48

Shawl Embroidered in Straight Stitch

A piece of lightweight wool fabric was embroidered in a straight stitch with silk buttonhole twist thread at its ends to be used as a shawl. The thread was wound on the bobbin because the thread was too heavy to pass through the machine, and, therefore, the work was performed on the "wrong side." (The finished side was facedown on the machine, and the back of the wool faced up while it was being worked.) Of course, when you are working on the wrong side, it is important to check frequently to make certain all stitches being formed on the underside are smooth and even. After a little practice, you can actually feel when something goes amiss on the underside. Puckering is one hazard of embroidering lightweight fabrics. Frequent steam ironing as well as properly adjusted top thread tension will help minimize puckering. Thin fabrics can also be backed with a piece of typing paper to add stiffness during sewing; the typing paper may be torn away afterward. Of course, interfacing may be used to add support where the back of an embroidered form will be hidden (as with a lining), but in this case no lining was used and the "underside" of the shawl was required to be as presentable as the face.

Animal Fiber V (31″ x 26″ x 3″), by Anna V. A. Polesný. Irregular pieces of suede machine-embroidered together edge to edge with the straight stitch to create a relief surface. Additional straight stitching defines the topography and adds subtle textural qualities to the piece. *Courtesy: Anna V. A. Polesný*

Very Female—Nudes on Canvas (32″ x 8″ x 15″), a canvas bag embroidered with the straight stitch by Joan Schulze. *Courtesy: Joan Schulze*

Satin-Stitch Place Mats

A set of fine pale blue polyester and cotton place mats was embroidered in variations on a single design theme. Designs were first sketched on paper. But they were executed on the fabric directly without the aid of actual tracing or transfer. Tailor's chalk and a ruler were, however, used to make certain that the lines of satin-stitch embroidery would be parallel where required. Polyester thread was used in a satin stitch of fixed width. Because multiple rows of zigzag stitching can cause puckering on light linen fabrics, the fabric was kept under fairly stiff tension during sewing to compensate. A steam iron was also used to eliminate minor puckering. After the designs had been embroidered, the fabric was cut to the proper dimensions for place mats (including an allowance for a hem) and hemmed.

51

Embroidered Velvet Jerkin

Printed fabrics may be accented with machine embroidery. Parts of this design will be "filled in" with a glossy silk machine thread using satin stitch and straight stitch. Skillful manipulation of the fabric and of the width of the satin stitch are required.

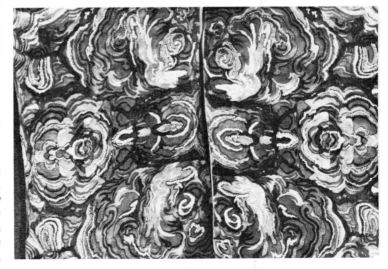

Embroidery of some areas of the printed design gives it a more varied texture. Symmetrical pieces of fabric are cut to size for the jerkin, with attention to the symmetry of the repeat designs in the print, so that the patterns on each side of the front of the vest will mirror each other.

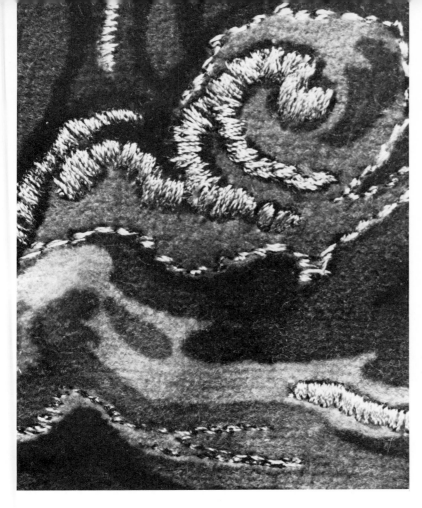

Since the shapes to be followed in satin stitch are irregular, maximum freedom to move the fabric is necessary and, as a sewing aid, the fabric is placed in an embroidery frame and made taut. The teeth or "dogs" under the plate, which move the fabric in one direction, are covered (some machines allow them to be lowered) so that they will not interfere with free movement of the fabric. It may also be possible to use an embroidery or darning foot or no foot at all. The top thread tension should be looser than normal, and the arm that usually lowers the presser foot must be in the "down" position in order to engage it and thereby engage the thread tension device. Stitch length is set at 0.

The first stitch in each section of embroidery accent is locked by bringing both the bobbin thread and the top thread to the back surface and tying them. During embroidery, sufficient downward pressure is applied to the fabric so that it remains close to the plate. Experiment with the various settings of thread tension so that you achieve a satin stitch that is visible in the pile of the velvet but that does not expose too much of the bobbin thread. Any direction of movement is possible during embroidery. Follow the contours of the velvet pattern and adjust the width of the satin stitch as necessary to suit the design. Fill in as much or as little of the printed pattern as you desire. A few tips on working with the silk thread on velvet: you may find that the silk threads will break. If they do, the tension may be too great, the thread may be caught on something, or perhaps the fabric is not being held flat to the plate. When fabric bobs up and down during sewing, it creates friction on the thread, causing it to fray, weaken, and break. If the fabric does bob up and down, try tightening the fabric in the embroidery hoop or using a presser foot or embroidery foot.

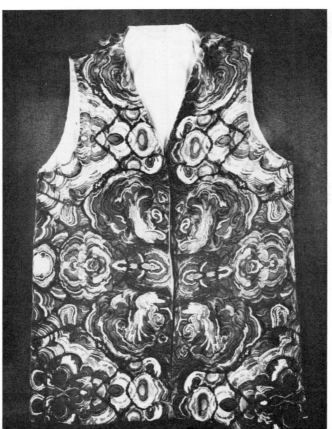

A dancer's bag by Ann Reilly in canvas embroidered in satin stitching of various colors.

A batik fabric machine-embroidered in straight stitch.

Tablecloth with Satin-stitch Border

A round yellow linen-textured polyester/cotton tablecloth was embroidered in satin stitch to create a looping border design. The design was first sketched on a piece of paper (center), and because the design was a repeat pattern—two loops and a scallop—one "unit" of the design was drawn to full scale (shown lying on the folded tablecloth).

54

Dressmaker's carbon paper (Dritz tracing paper) was placed directly over the fabric, the design unit was placed over the carbon, and the design was traced. The position of each design unit was determined by measuring with a ruler from the outside edge of the cloth.

The design unit was traced repeatedly around the border of the fabric, using carbon paper. The sections must be aligned—which required care. As an aid in positioning the paper pattern, guidelines were drawn on the fabric with tailor's chalk. Never draw directly on the carbon paper—it is thin and tears easily.

As in all designs requiring a smooth satin stitch, it is important to know how to produce an even satin stitch on a particular type of fabric. Always practice on the specific fabric, especially where, as here, special shapes (repeated circles) will be sewn. Polyester thread was used in this zigzag stitch, at a fixed width with normal top tension. A clear plastic presser foot, which allows one to see every stitch as it is made, was used. One important tip when working with large pieces of fabric: do not allow the fabric to hang from the machine. Hanging causes distortion of the embroidery and weave. Keep unwieldy lengths of fabric folded in your lap or on a table behind the machine so that the weight is not on the needle or on the embroidery.

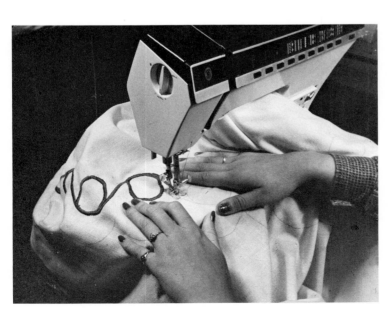

The outer scallop edge of the embroidery was embroidered in polyester thread of a different color. The belly of each scallop was a fixed stitch width, but the stitch width was tapered as peaks in the scallop were approached. Practice making a smooth tapered satin stitch on scrap fabric. Hold the fabric taut between thumb and index finger as you feed it through the machine. Use your free hand to gradually dial narrower and narrower stitch settings. It takes a little practice to become truly proficient at the graduated satin stitch. One of the hardest skills to learn is keeping it even so that stitches do not overlap but also do not have gaps between them.

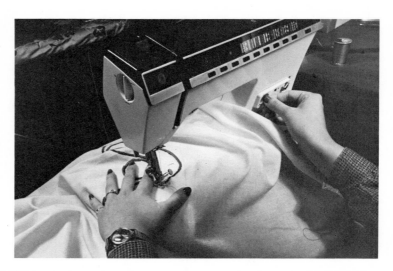

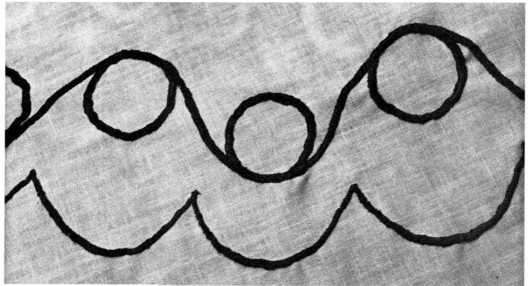

A close-up of the completed border design.

Chalk marks disappeared with the first washing. The finished tablecloth is yellow, with embroidery in turquoise and tan.

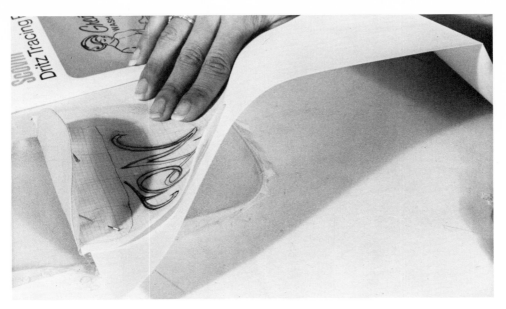

Monograms

The satin stitch is most typically used in monogramming, but it is also possible to use many other stitches. Satin stitch can also be used to outline initials. The bead, ribbon, and arrowhead stitches can all be used to design initials. To begin, find an attractive way of arranging the initials. Try script or block letters, or look for inspirations in magazines, old books, and manuals on lettering. Several companies manufacture monogram letters ready to be ironed onto fabric as a basis for embroidery. These iron-ons (and another type made for use with the Pressure-Fax transfer pen) can be found in most fabric stores. The original sketch of a monogram shown in this picture is going to be transferred to the pocket of a blouse. The pocket was removed from the blouse, and separated from its lining. To transfer the "TRN" monogram to the fabric, a sheet of dressmaker's carbon paper has been sandwiched between sketch and pocket.

The sketch was traced firmly to transfer carbon from the paper to the pocket.

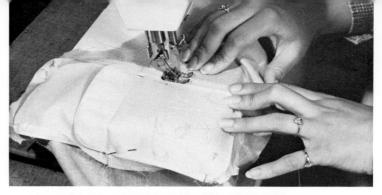

Monograms should be embroidered using an embroidery hoop, but this pocket was too small to fit on a hoop, so it was basted onto a large piece of fabric which would fit in the hoop.

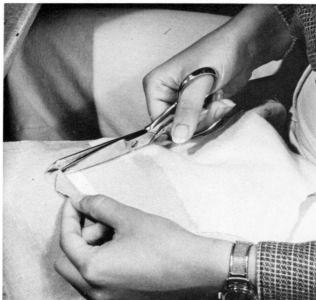

A window was cut in the backing so that it would not be sewn to the pocket.

The monogram was embroidered without a presser foot. The threads were first pulled to the top of the fabric, and the first stitch was locked into place.

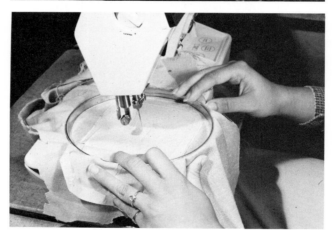

The satin-stitched monogram should be smooth and even. Practice is, once again, the key to success. A graduated satin stitch was used.

58

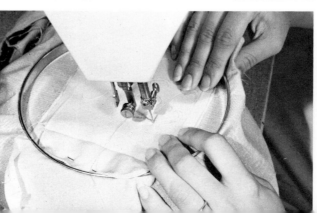

When the satin-stitch monogram was finished, the pocket liner was re-inserted and the pocket was re-stitched to the blouse.

Guest Towels

The principle here is simple but worth remembering. If it is not convenient to embroider directly on a particular piece of fabric, it is often possible to embroider on a separate piece of fabric and then appliqué the one fabric to the other. Terry cloth towels have such a deep pile that almost any embroidery would get lost in it. Therefore, a band of washable cotton fabric was embroidered with red roses in a spiraling bead stitch. The stitching began from the center of the rose and the cotton was turned constantly to produce a flower. The decorative leaf stitching was then added.

The rose and leaf bands were first attached to the towels with a straight stitch and finished with the zigzag stitch in silver metallic thread. The edges of the bands were folded back and ironed before sewing both to make sewing easier and to make certain that no stray frayed edges would break through.

59

Velvet Belt with Metallic Thread

An elegant, dressy look can be produced on velvet by embroidering with metallic thread. Velvet is notorious, however, for obscuring embroidery in its pile. If thread tension is too great, threads will "sink" and almost disappear. One way to help bring out the stitches is to work on velvet backed by a piece of paper. This helps stitches stand taller in the fabric. In this particular block design, it was necessary to count the length of each automatic stitch, to see how to fit all stitches without having to cut any off in mid-stitch. The bead and honeycomb stitches used here turn corners well if the needle is left in the fabric. The embroidery foot is lifted, the fabric rotated 90 degrees, the foot lowered, and the sewing continued. The Greek key stitch, however, does not turn corners as well. One must stop the stitch at the end of the row and start again after the corner has been turned.

Most of the paper backing was torn away after embroidering. If desired, the belt can be lined with another fabric to hide the wrong-side stitchery.

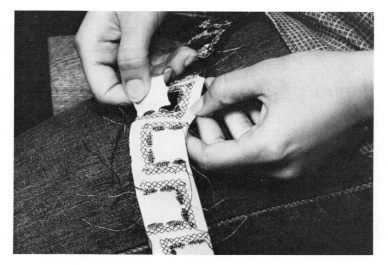

The edges of the belt were finished with very narrow satin stitch.

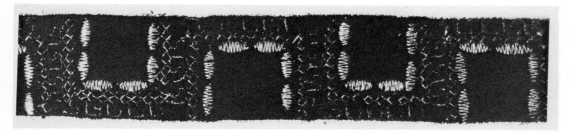

The belt was completed by hand sewing a fancy buckle at one end.

Linen Garden Skirt

After you have practiced the various stitches and have explored some creative ways of altering their appearance, it is easy to create unique embroidery using combinations of stitches. Skirt borders may be embroidered before the skirt is sewn or after, by letting down the hem. Designs for five or six different flowers, wheat, and grass were developed on scrap fabric. Tailor's chalk was used to sketch a few on the linen, but most of the designs were sewn as inspiration struck. *Wheat* was a tapering satin-stitch stalk, zigzag stem, and bead stitch for the grains. To make these grains, the beads were first stitched loosely with a long stitch and were then sewn over a second time with a shorter stitch to add some depth to each grain. The short flowers were short zigzag stems, with arrowhead stitches for leaves and random multicolor zigzag as the flowers themselves. The Touch-Tronic 2000 has a handy option: by pressing a special button a single automatic stitch can be produced. This option was used to make leaves of a single arrowhead stitch. Blades of grass were composed of light featherstitch. A combination of leaf stitch with tulip stitch became the leafy, middle-height stalks.

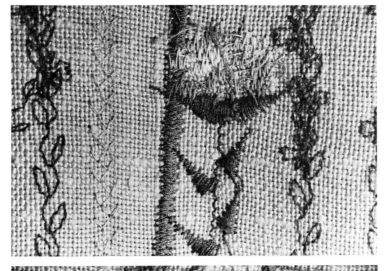

Close-up of *(from left):* leaf-stitch stem; featherstitch grass; satin-stitch stem for a wheat design; flower made of zigzag stem, arrowhead leaves, random zigzag flower; leaf stitch with tulip stitch.

Close-up of wheat grains showing the combination of zigzag, loosely sewn bead stitches (with very long stitch-length setting), and tightly sewn bead stitches.

Linen garden skirt by Thelma
R. Newman.

Afghani Embroidered Shirt

In Kandahar, Afghanistan, and
elsewhere in central Asia,
elaborately embroidered shirts
and long robes are sold in
bazaars and shops. In even the
smallest shops men can often
be seen sitting at sewing
machines, creating machine
embroidery in traditional
patterns using programmed
stitches. They also do free-
motion embroidery, using a
hoop wrapped in fabric so that
material will not slip and
loosen in the hoop.

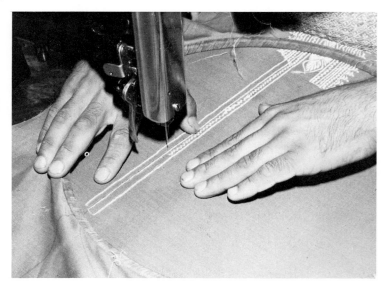

62

The man working at the machine is also wearing one of his own creations. Designs are most often embroidered on finely woven lightweight cottons using silk machine-embroidery thread from India and Pakistan. Note that two hands are used to guide the fabric and keep it taut near the needle.

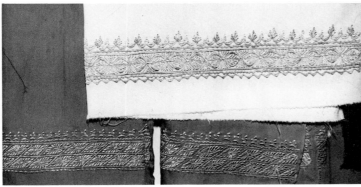

Embroidery for sleeve cuffs and shirt fronts from Kandahar, Afghanistan, prior to being sewn into clothing.

63

Ribbon Pillow

Machine stitchery can be used to create a patterned fabric out of ribbons and scraps. Here a variety of stitches were used to attach overlapping widths of grosgrain ribbon. This kind of work is easier if you use one type of ribbon (so you needn't contend with different grains). Shown here are the elastic stretch, ricrac, honeycomb, feather, and overedge stitches.

The only difficulty in sewing the ribbons is keeping them straight. Using lots of pins will help keep the ribbons secure. Press with an iron after a few ribbons have been stitched together to keep puckering to a minimum. Shown here: ricrac and honeycomb stitches.

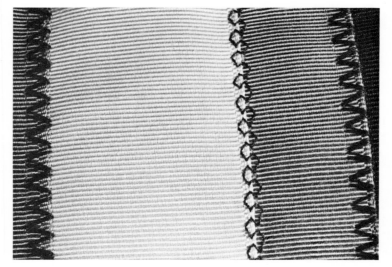

The finished pillow with an edge of grosgrain ribbon over cording.

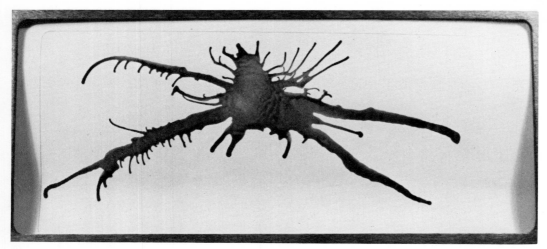

Ink-blot Serving Tray

In much the same way that the velvet jerkin was embroidered in the satin stitch, this random ink pattern was filled with the "darning stitch." Other stitches could also have been used. India ink was dropped on paper and blown in different directions to create a random-looking design that fit within the limits of the serving tray. The tray was part of a special kit that included the wood frame and glass to frame any piece of fabric. Similar kits are available at many fabric and crafts stores. Assorted pocketbooks, appointment calendar books, coin purses, and other useful items are manufactured with the needleworker in mind.

A special transfer material called Pressure-Fax (made by Graphic Techniques Company, Dayton, Ohio) was used to transfer the design from paper to fabric. Pressure-Fax transfer paper was first placed over the design and taped securely to prevent movement. The design was traced with a special transfer pen.

The transfer paper was then placed, face down, on the fabric to be embroidered and rubbed, over its entire surface, with a fingernail or a burnishing tool or the side of a spoon.

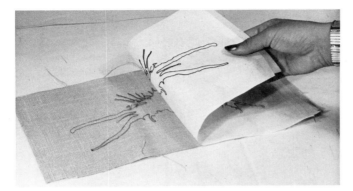

Before the transfer paper was removed, it was lifted to reveal whether all the design had been successfully transferred. Pressure-Fax produces its strongest image if used within one hour of inking. More than one image can be transferred using a single inked pattern.

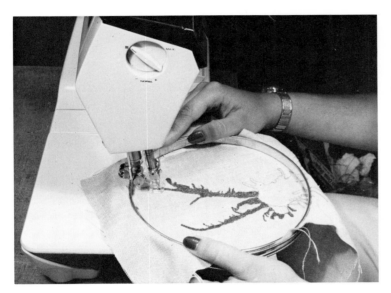

A darning stitch was used to fill the transferred outline. The machine was set for darning, the darning foot was attached, and the normal needle plate was replaced with a plate that covered the feed dogs. On some machines, the dogs are lowered. The machine was set for straight stitch with a stitch length of 0. The fabric was embroidered in a hoop.

The completed embroidery was centered in the tray's frame and secured by stapling. Fabric may also be secured by taping it or by hand sewing it in place.

Big Apple Bag

A large felt bag was designed by Thelma R. Newman of red felt (apple), green felt (leaves), brown felt (stem-handle), and white felt (lining). She began by making a paper mock-up of the bag. The paper pieces were used as templates for cutting the felt. Paper was pinned to double-thickness felt (since two faces of both red and white were required). The felt was cut with shears, and allowance was made for a hem. The white liner should be cut ¼″ smaller than the outer part of the bag, so that it will fit inside without bunching.

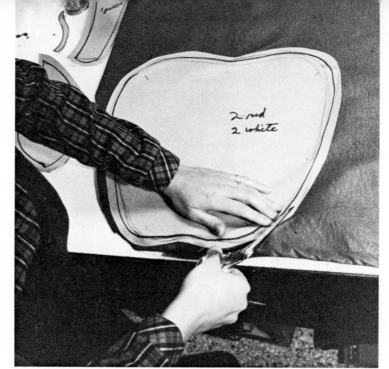

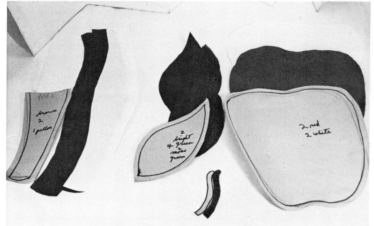

Shown here are *(from left):* the folded template for the stem with two brown felt pieces and a strip of Pellon (iron-on interfacing); light- and moss-green leaves; felt worm; and the red felt apple and its white lining.

Patterns radiating out from the base and stem of the apple were drawn with tailor's chalk.

68

Those patterns were embroidered in featherstitch in several colors of polyester thread following the tailor's chalk guidelines. Lighter colors were used nearer the bottom of the apple.

A brown felt worm stuffed with a small length of polyester filler material was attached to the apple bag with the zigzag stitch.

The leaves were marked for embroidery with tailor's chalk.

69

All four leaf surfaces were embroidered with the satin stitch before they were sewn together inside out. Before completing the seam, the leaves were turned right side out.

A two-inch-wide felt gusset was made for the entire length of the outer edge of the apple liner and sewn into place.

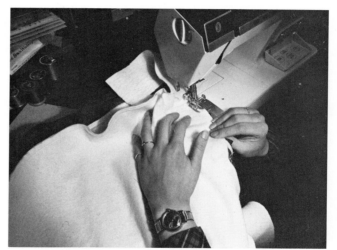

The completed liner with gusset around three sides.

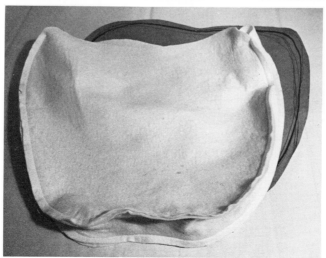

70

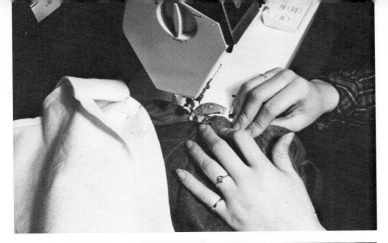

The leaves were next sewn into place near the top of the apple, as was the stem handle.

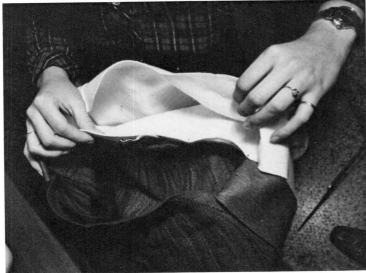

The lining was pinned to the top edge of the apple bag, leaving a margin for the seam. It was important that when the lining was inside the bag, the unfinished edges be hidden. The lining was sewn in place, leaving one side open. The lining was pushed inside the bag and a slip stitch was used to close the rest of the top edge of the bag.

"Big Apple" bag by Thelma R. Newman.

71

Machine Lace

Intricate lace can be created on a sewing machine. A fine example by Niloofer Daver is shown here. In essence, machine lace uses fabric or parts of fabric as a framework. The fabric may be removed and the machine embroidery will remain. Machine lace is usually begun by defining the outer edge of the form with several rows of zigzag stitching. Other areas are defined in a similar manner. Fabric within such areas may then be cut away with a sharp scissors. With covered or lowered feed dogs, a darning or embroidery foot, and stitch length set at zero, the interweaving of fine strands of thread characteristic of lace may begin. After anchoring the thread in the wall of your framework with a few stitches, thread must be released from the spool and bobbin so that it may be stretched across the framework to another point where it will also be anchored. Thread may be released by simply lifting the presser bar so that thread will be played out as you pull (because top thread tension will have been removed), or some machines may be fooled into thinking that fabric is in place so that thread will be released when pulled while "sewing" quickly. Of course, threads may be crisscrossed and sewn over and otherwise manipulated and combined. In addition, specialty stitches such as the zigzag stitch may be used to bind groups of single strands. Note as well that although organza was used here, many fabrics are suitable for machine lacework, and it is not necessary to cut all the fabric away. Lacework may be combined with solid areas of fabric too.

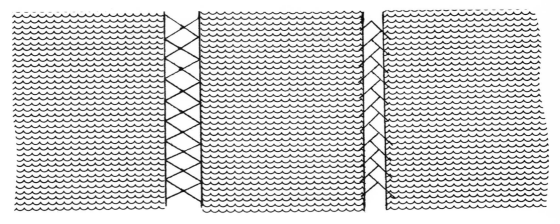

Faggoted Tablecloth

Machine faggoting is a method by which automatic stitches may be used to delicately connect two pieces of fabric edge to edge. The two pieces of fabric are placed about ¼″ apart, parallel to each other, and pinned to a strip of paper underneath the fabrics so that the gap between the two pieces of fabric is bridged. The edge of each piece of fabric is then followed with a zigzag stitch so that the zigzags overlap slightly in the middle, and when the paper is pulled away the two rows of zigzag stitching have intertwined to attach the pieces of fabric, as shown above, left. The featherstitch can also be used to produce a faggoted effect, as shown above, right. This tablecloth was planned with cut paper. An eight-pointed star was created which could be folded into sections.

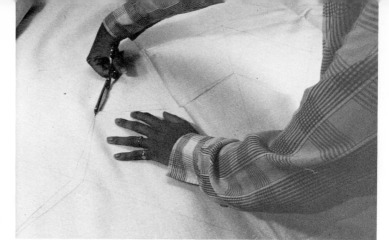

The idea was translated into cloth and cut.

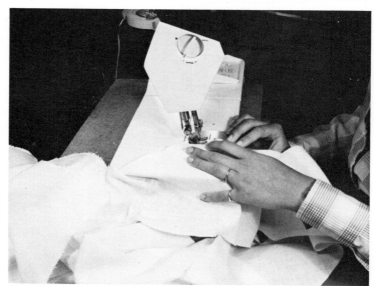

All cloth edges were overedged.

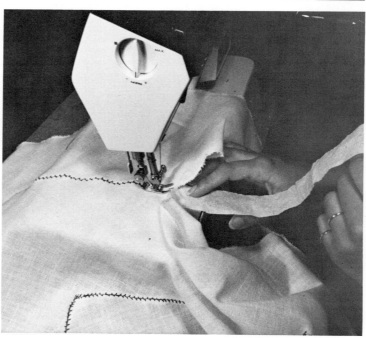

The featherstitch was used to faggot and directly connect both pieces of fabric in one pass. Note how the strip of paper is used to bridge the gap between the edges of the fabric. Before diving into this project, practice to see how wide a stitch is needed to leave sufficient space between fabrics.

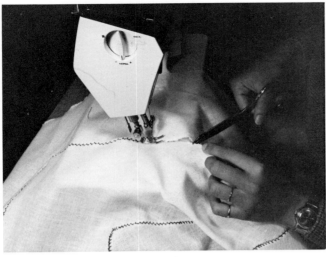

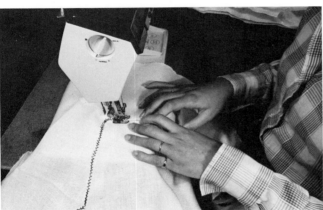

Fabric is clipped to make it easier to turn corners.

Machine-faggoted tablecloth by Thelma R. Newman.

75

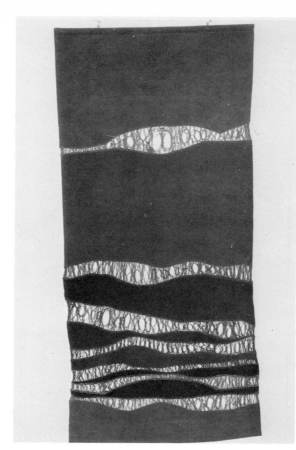

Animal Fiber XIV (26″ x 60″), by Anna V. A. Polesný, a wall piece of suede and machine lacework of cotton thread.

A close-up of *Animal Fiber XIV,* showing machine lacework, by Anna V. A. Polesný.

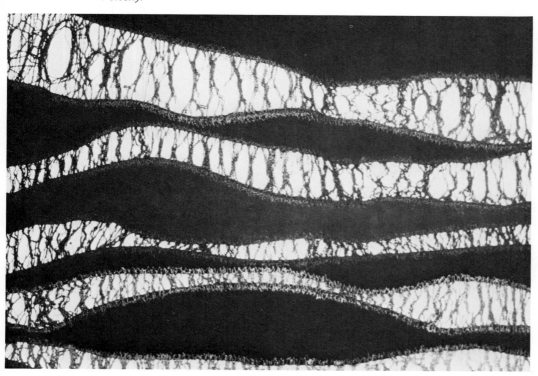

Animal Fiber XI (39″ x 70″),
another wall piece of suede
and machine lacework by Anna
V. A. Polesný.

A close-up of *Animal Fiber XI*.
*Photos courtesy Anna V. A.
Polesný*

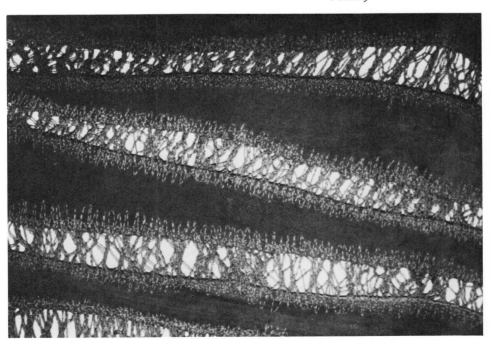

Harvest (5' x 9'), appliquéd hanging by Margaret Cusack, commissioned by architect George Nelson. *Courtesy: Margaret Cusack; photo by eeva-inkeri*

3

MACHINE APPLIQUÉ

ABOUT APPLIQUÉ

Remarkable appliqué—the clever patch on a pauper's coat, the elegant design on a king's or prelate's garment—has meant many things to many people. The magic of a shape, a few embroidery stitches, fanciful and plain fabrics, simple and elegant yarns, may be combined in appliqué. Successful design in appliqué depends on subtle modeling of light as well as juxtaposition of colors, shapes, and textures. The play of light on different textiles is modified by stitching and embroidery. Appliqué is a personal and vital art form as well as a practical way of manipulating fabric.

The word "appliqué" comes from the French *appliquer*, meaning "to put" or "to lay on." And that is just what appliqué is: the technique of applying fabric cutouts to a background. This is distinguished from patchwork, which is the simple joining of one juxtaposed piece to another. The two techniques work well together.

Appliqué has known many interpretations over the years, and many distinct styles have emerged. For example, some standard appliqué quilt patterns, such as Whig Rose, Oak Leaf Wreath, and Ohio Rose, have

Epsolini (7″ x 14″) is one in a series of highly decorated suede clown bags by Anna V. A. Polesný that combines machine embroidery for appliqué, structure, and decoration. The bag was also machine-beaded. *Courtesy: Anna V. A. Polesný; photo by Anna V. A. Polesný*

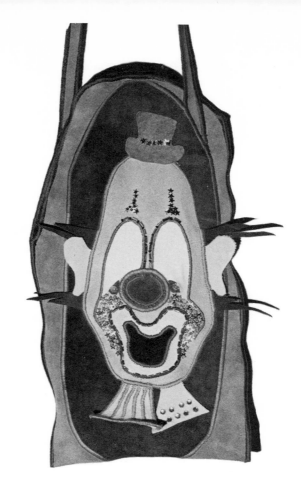

Mysterie (35″ x 32″), a machine-embroidered and -appliquéd wall hanging by Doreen Lah. *Courtesy: Doreen Lah; photo by Doreen Lah*

come down to us. Reverse appliqué, which involves cutting into stacked layers of fabric to reveal new layers underneath, is a technique that was adopted by the Cuna Indian women of Panama and Colombia to make their *molas* (blouses). The *kapa pohopoko* and *kapa lau* emerged in Hawaii when New England missionaries introduced the technique of piecing squares together. Hawaiian women uniquely interpreted the original version with their wave quilting *(luma lau)*. *Broderie perse* was the cutting apart of integral shapes, fruit, flowers, birds—originally from Indian *palampores*—and reassembling these figures in a new interpretation on another background. Banners—as temporary, free-flowing fabric forms used to celebrate an event—employ unique symbolism and appliqué styles. New interpretations are still emerging as a plethora of textiles and a new generation of sewing machines are combined in appliqué and embroidery. Appliqué even lends itself to serious picture making—painting with fabrics and stitches.

PLANNING AND DESIGNING

There are many approaches to the design of appliqué. One is to work spontaneously—directly with fabric and stitches on a background, without formal planning. Another is to carefully design the piece and work strictly from that original conception. Of course, even working directly with materials actually involves planning, however informal. You are continually faced with choices as to fabrics, threads, whether to use machine processes alone, or to use hand processes as well. You must consider the piece's function and purpose, overall size and style of the work, and of course, the shapes and textures to be created.

In the formal approach, planning begins with pencil and paper sketches or with cut paper to lay out a design. One can also begin with a sketch and later translate it to paper. Whatever can be cut from paper can be cut from fabric as well, making this a good approach to the creation of appliqué.

Almost any subject matter can serve as an inspiration for appliqué—geometric forms, natural forms, fantasies, abstractions. Many relationships between pieces to be appliquéd must be considered: spaces between shapes; overlapping of shapes; the function and juxtaposition of texture to color, color to color, and color to shape; the purposes of lines (sewn and embroidered); use of color lines; repetition of lines to create pattern and provide definition. All these possibilities must be considered, and therein lies the creative aspect of appliqué.

Couched Yarns on Velvet

Cords and yarns are exceptionally well-suited for appliqué because they offer great design flexibility and may be sewed to fabric easily. The process of sewing cords or yarn to fabric is referred to as "couching" or "cording." It is sometimes said that couching involves tacking a cord or yarn to fabric with an under thread (as with a zigzag stitch), and that cording involves the sewing of cord or yarn to fabric (as with a straight stitch). Couching can involve the use of yarn or cord as an intermediate step, as when cord or yarn is covered completely with satin stitching or fabric to achieve a raised effect. Cording, on the other hand, would describe only the application of yarn or cord as a primary decorative element. In this design, hand-held fluffy yarn is being applied to velvet.

The stitch used to attach it should be as wide as the yarn. Yarn must be centered under the stitch. Pins may be used to align the yarn. To turn a corner, leave the needle in the fabric at the inside of the corner, lift the presser foot and pivot the fabric around the needle. To add more cord or to connect yarns end to end, slightly overlap the cord ends. Stitch over both ends to couch them together.

82

The top and bottom threads should be pulled to the back of the fabric and tied.

The completed design in shades of green and blue yarn couched on blue velvet was made into a couch pillow.

Wrap-around Skirt Decorated in Couched Silk Cord

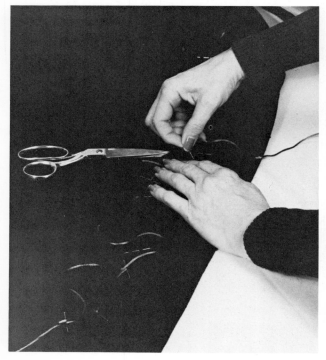

Floral designs in silk satin cord are shown being pinned to the front and border of a wrap-around skirt of matte black wool. The shiny cord contrasts nicely with the matte surface of the wool. The pins hold the satin cord in place while the design is being planned. Of course, once the design has been laid out on the fabric, the pins will serve as a sewing aid.

This close-up shows part of the design, a flowing pattern of floral forms.

Free-embroidered (straight and zigzag stitches) leaflike elements punctuate the meandering stem.

This magnified view of one of the "flowers" shows that each piece of silk satin cord is couched with zigzag stitch formed of silk machine thread. The strands of cord used in the flowers are four shades of yellow and orange. A special-purpose machine foot made to accommodate cording of this diameter was used to faciliate the couching. Do not let the confluence of yarns make the base of the flower too bulky or it will be difficult to sew and the needle may bend or break.

Thelma R. Newman's floral motif extends around the bottom of the skirt and up the front.

85

The neckline, sleeve cuffs, and pocket of this robe were corded for decoration. Moroccan cord, a braidlike cord, was applied with a straight stitch using invisible nylon thread.

A detail of the Moroccan cord pocket decoration.

86

Machine-couched silk cord on
batik cotton fabric.

Top-couched Bottom-corded Ultrasuede® Pillow

To understand where the following steps will lead you, study the finished pillow first. Brown cord was first machine-couched to the face of beige Ultrasuede. The brown cord was too thick to be passed through the machine as top thread but not too thick to pass through the machine as bobbin thread, so it was wound onto the bobbin by hand. The fabric will be sewn facedown (with reduced top-thread tension) so that the bobbin thread will appear as a line of couched thread on the face of the Ultrasuede.

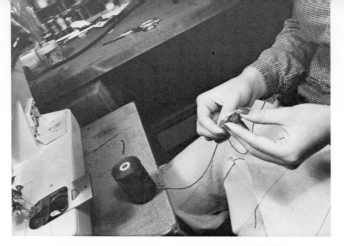

A diagonal grid of brown cord is sewn onto a square piece of beige Ultrasuede. Since the "wrong" side (the side that will be on the inside of the pillow) will face up during sewing, the grid pattern to be sewn was sketched in pencil. Enough brown cord was wound onto the bobbin prior to sewing each line of the grid so that each line would be continuous (and not marred by unsightly breaks).

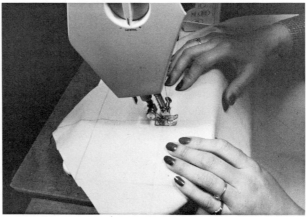

The face of the Ultrasuede is occasionally turned up during sewing to check on the couching of the brown cord. The pencil lines marking the grid to be sewn are visible.

Even with reduced top-thread tension, the Ultrasuede may pucker slightly during sewing. Ultrasuede is somewhat elastic and may stretch a bit during sewing. To correct this puckering an extra length of brown cord is left at one end of each line of the grid and the fabric is pulled gently to remove the pucker.

88

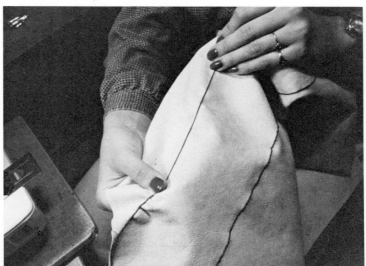

After the grid of brown cord is reverse-couched onto the face of the Ultrasuede, the Ultrasuede is placed face up over a sheet of broadcloth that will become its backing. The broadcloth base for the Ultrasuede helps to throw the Ultrasuede into relief over cotton cording. As illustrated, the cording is placed between the Ultrasuede and the broadcloth backing and held in place with straight pins. The face of the Ultrasuede is then marked lightly with tailor's chalk to indicate both sides of the cording.

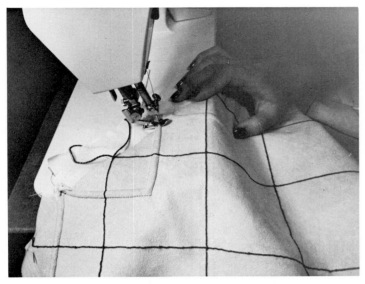

The Ultrasuede and broadcloth backing are then straight-stitched together in brown thread along a chalk-marked line indicating one side of cording. The cording is then placed between the Ultrasuede and backing so that the backing is flat and the Ultrasuede forms a line in relief over the cording. The Ultrasuede and backing are again sewn together to lock the cording between them.

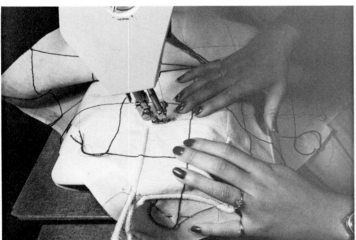

A zipper foot is used in sewing the second row of straight stitching to lock in the cording. This allows the Ultrasuede to conform firmly around the cording. The straight stitching is placed as close to the cording as possible. It is absolutely imperative that the backing be kept taut during this step in the process so that only the Ultrasuede is raised in relief. Note, as well, that the cording itself does not naturally form the crisp right angle shown. Rather, the angle is created by stitching the channel as desired; the cording gradually conforms to the proper shape afterward.

This close-up shows the Ultrasuede with couched brown cord, straight-stitched to a broadcloth backing over cotton cord to throw the Ultrasuede into relief.

The finished material was sewn to Ultrasuede piping created by sewing a strip of Ultrasuede over cording. The piped pillow face was then sewn to a piece of undecorated Ultrasuede backed in broadcloth.

The finished pillow, by Thelma R. Newman, is a study in relationships among space, shadow, and shape. The darkness of the brown cording contrasts with the subtle modeling of the Ultrasuede created by the hidden cording. The shapes created by the grid of brown cording echo and redefine the shapes created by the zigzag of the relief.

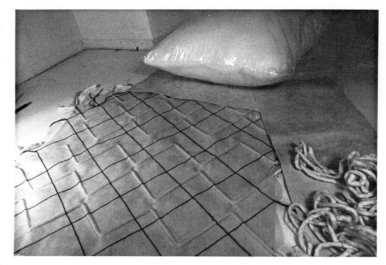

90

TRANSFER OF DESIGN

Designs may be transferred from paper to paper or from paper to fabric in many ways. These ways have been discussed and demonstrated in Chapter 1, and are applicable in appliqué as in any embroidery.

FABRIC

The qualities of the fabrics used in appliqué play crucial roles in the success of the design. It is helpful to think about each fabric in two general ways: its working characteristics and its aesthetic characteristics.

Working characteristics are those that relate to the way in which a fabric performs *physically*. Is it easy to sew? Does it iron easily? Does it wear well? How does it handle the different embroidery stitches? Generally, firm, closely woven fabrics are the easiest to sew. Natural fabrics, such as cottons, linens, and wools, iron the easiest and, in addition, lie flatter and pucker less than synthetics. Fabric "grain" should be considered, especially when loose weaves are used. If the grain is twisted the fabric usually won't lie flat. Nearly all fabrics can be made easier to work with through the addition of a second layer of support or reinforcement. The use of a backing fabric will prevent, or at least reduce, stretching, puckering, and pulling. Organza and organdy are often basted to the back of a fabric to provide support. A fusible material, such as Pellon, may also be used quite effectively. Tissue paper or typing paper placed behind fabric while it is being sewn also can provide support and can, in many cases, be removed after sewing.

Aesthetic characteristics are, for most people, the single most significant aspect of using fabrics. Some fabrics are hard to work with but aesthetically are right for the piece being created, justifying the struggle.

It is not easy to define the aesthetic characteristics

91

of a fabric. But it is possible to describe a few elements related to the appearance of a fabric which help determine whether a fabric is suitable for a particular application.

Significant elements of fabric design include:

• *Pattern:* a fabric may have a distinct pattern as a result of the way in which it was woven. Patterns in solid fabrics may take the form of predominant lines running in the direction of either warp or weft, lines running on a bias, or subtle repeat designs that result from variations in the weave. Pattern can be distorted by pulling holes in loose weaves like hessian and linen scrim. In fabrics woven in more than one color, pattern is a function of how the threads blend or compete, highlighting one or another of the colors. Printed fabrics can make designing more difficult. Printed patterns can overwhelm your own designs. The trick is to find ways of working the print into your scheme.

• *Texture:* Like pattern, texture can be entirely dependent on the way in which fabric is woven. But probably more significant than the weave is the thread or yarn that is used. A fabric woven of very fine cotton or silk thread usually has an even, smooth texture. A fabric woven of raw silk, hemp, or heavy yarn will often appear rougher, more uneven. The slubs stick out of the fabric in random rhythm. Diagonal weaves (twill) add another textural quality.

• *Color:* Once mentioned, it would appear to be impossible to say enough about color without saying too much. Suffice it to say that color, and combinations of colors, are extremely important considerations. If you are uncomfortable with selecting "compatible" colors, you can stick to familiar color groupings—cool colors of blue, green, turquoise; warm colors of red, yellow and orange; "neutral" colors of brown, tan, gray, black, and white.

• *Reflectance:* The degree to which a fabric reflects light is an important design consideration, although it is rarely recognized as such. Fabrics, like all objects, reflect light to different degrees and in different ways. The result is that some appear to be shiny or glossy like satin, and others appear to be dull or matte like felt. Glossy fabrics may look more formal than duller fabrics, and tightly woven materials may be thought to look more formal than the more loosely woven fabrics that use heavier yarns.

How are such factors relevant to designing for appliqué or machine embroidery? The goal in appliqué, as in designing anything, is to produce an integrated work that is as exciting or subdued as the designer desires. Think carefully about how the *lines* within each fabric relate to those in other fabrics—and how the lines created by positioning each fabric swatch beside another fit within the piece as a whole. Think of how the *textures* of the various fabrics relate to each other—just as you would think about whether different colors "match" or contrast. See how highly textured fabrics interact with those that are smooth and even. At the same time, experiment with ways glossy fabrics relate to matte fabrics. In the same vein, think about whether a particular fabric requires a stronger design. Heavy fabrics, for instance, usually will require boldness. Intricate and subtle patterns will be more effective with refined fabrics. Thread choice will be an important consideration when combining appliqué and embroidery. Fine threads will be buried in deep pile like terry cloth or thick fabric like corduroy. Rough or bulky cording may distort or clash with fine silks or soft cottons. Most important: keep playing with different combinations.

One of the best ways to stretch your capacity to design with fabric is to accumulate a wide variety of materials and work with them. Look for smooth cottons, rough cottons, smooth wools, rough wools, deep-pile velvets and velveteens, fine silks and slub silks, burlap, gauzes, open-mesh muslins, organdies, felts, loosely woven hessian, scrim, twills and worsteds, plastics—clear, colored, transparent, opaque, and translucent. Don't stop scrounging for exciting and soothing textures. Generate a library of fabrics and experiment: pull out threads, back them, unback them, stretch them, double them, quilt them, tuft them. Combine patterns with patterns, tufted fabrics with vinyls, leathers with silks, gauzes with velvets—but do not expect all your efforts to pan out! Expect them to open you to new possibilities. Attempt to define precisely what you want to create in the process.

CUTTING AND ATTACHING SHAPES

Using sharp, pointed scissors at least four inches long, cut along the outlines of your pieces. If the fabric tends to fray, there are several ways to deal with it: cut it with a pinking shears, temporarily attach masking tape to the edges (remove before sewing), spray the piece with spray starch, or sew along the edges with a hand or machine basting stitch.

After the pieces have been cut, they are ready to be arranged and mounted. A very handy way, as a preliminary step, is to tack the pieces with pins on a *tack board* as they would finally appear in the finished piece. Arrange and rearrange pieces as much as you like. Tack boards may be cork bulletin boards, rigid corrugated boards such as portable cutting boards (purchased in sewing supply centers), foam core boards (a sandwich of two pieces of cardboard with a filler of rigid foam) or expanded flat Styrofoam® panels.

Next, the shapes are transferred and attached to the foundation fabric. The fabric may be mounted in a frame or spread out on a table unattached. (If you are using a frame, allow a margin of several inches.) Attachment is a *critical* step. Secure all pieces of fabric as well as possible before sewing or embroidering. When first starting out, you may find that a fusible interfacing material, like Poly-Web® or Stitchwitchery®, holds fabric better than pinning would. Take advantage of these technical advances. After pinning or fusing pieces, baste the fabrics to be appliquéd to the foundation fabric. Well-secured fabrics are easier to embroider.

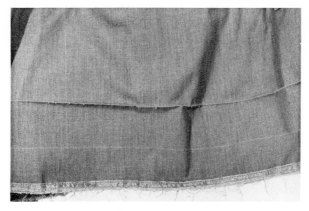

Nearly any material may be applied to another material with machine stitching. And appliqué may serve utilitarian as well as decorative purposes. Consider, for example, the waste caused by longer skirt lengths. Unsightly hemlines can be camouflaged . . .

. . . by straight stitching rows of scalloped trim ricrac around the border of the skirt.

95

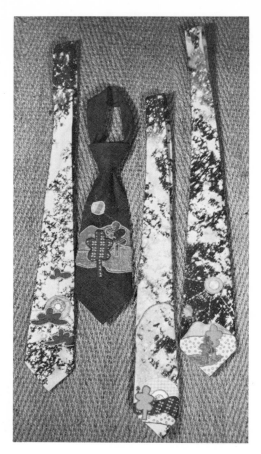

Four ties by Ellen Tobey
Holmes machine-appliquéd in
satin stitch. *Courtesy: The
Handworks Gallery, New York*

Fabrics may be appliquéd
without having been
temporarily fastened
beforehand. But most often
pieces to be appliquéd are
attached first with straight pins
or by basting. After sewing,
pins or basting may be
removed.

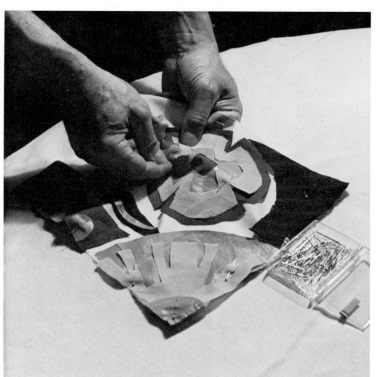

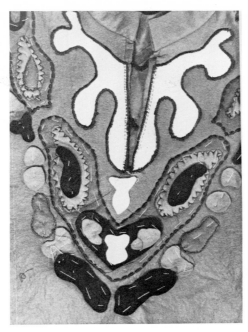

Prior to sewing, pieces of felt
to be appliquéd were basted to
hold them in place. Bead, satin,
and scallop stitches were used
to attach them to the felt top.

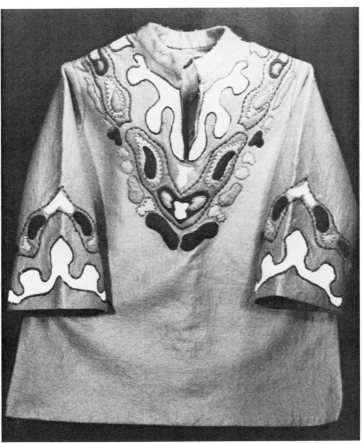

Gloria L. Bubeck machine appliquéd calico fabrics using the satin stitch to create *Saturday Night in the Kitchen* and *Bundling. Courtesy: Gloria L. Bubeck*

Tina Bobker and Carole Dlugasch of Rainbow Artisans, Inc., render homes and rooms in appliqué on request. *Courtesy: Rainbow Artisans, Inc.*

99

Tina Bobker and Carole Dlugasch first photograph the scene, home, or room to be re-created in fabric.

They then reduce the setting to its essential elements in order to make an appliqué rendering practical, and carefully choose fabrics and stitches in order to render the design in machine appliqué and machine embroidery. *Courtesy: Rainbow Artisans, Inc.*

Ann Reilly designed and sewed this jeans and jacket outfit for a child and machine appliquéd flowers of linen and polyester and cotton fabrics to the brushed denim jeans with a spread zigzag stitch.

A machine-appliquéd portrait pillow stuffed with polyester filler, by Margaret Cusack.

SEWING AND EMBROIDERING THE APPLIQUÉ

Given the host of embroidery stitches already explored in this book, almost any stitching or design problem can be solved.

To machine appliqué, baste your pieces to the background. It is usually not necessary to turn edges under in machine sewing. Outline the appliqué with short straight stitches. Remove the basting. Set the pattern selector for the embroidery pattern you wish—zigzag, featherstitch, or whatever, and adjust the stitch width to suit the thickness of the fabric. A wider stitch is probably more appropriate for a thick fabric. Adjust the stitch length to the desired setting. Then proceed to outline the entire edge of each piece with the stitch you have selected.

A second approach may also be used. The appliqué shape is not cut to the exact dimensions until *after* the shape has been sewn to the foundation fabric. After the shape has been secured, excess fabric is trimmed with an embroidery scissors.

DIRECTIONS IN APPLIQUÉ

All the many varieties of machine embroidery may be combined with appliqué. The possibilities are extraordinarily vast when the two are combined. Consider building on some of the traditional and contemporary variants of appliqué.

Persian embroidery or *broderie perse,* for example, is a form of art resembling decoupage, inasmuch as both were derived from Asiatic influence and both involve the cutting out of forms and applying them to a background. But instead of glue or paper, fabric and stitches are employed.

In the early 1700s, an act of Parliament prohibited the importation of Indian printed and painted calico known as *palampores.* As the prototypes of European printed calicos in the nineteenth century, printed and painted Indian bedcovers and prayer rugs became very precious indeed. The smallest scraps were considered valuable and were saved for patchwork and appliqué. Parts of these *palampores* were cut apart, rearranged, and appliquéd onto bleached and unbleached muslins and linens. Flowers, fruit trees, and other images were appliquéd with buttonhole and featherstitching.

Perse became another name for calico. However, this technique was probably called *broderie perse* because in Persia there was a type of embroidery that utilized odd bits of cloth by applying them to a base material (usually linen) with chain stitching. Also, the richly embellished embroideries of Persia were known in Europe and were often called *gilets persans* or *nakshe,* meaning ornament. They were extremely beautiful, elegant pieces.

Cutting apart fabric patterns and rearranging them into new appliqué forms has great possibility. So does cutting fabrics and rearranging them into portraits, scenes, still-life arrangements.

Consider banners as well. Banners were once used as temporary announcements—hanging from poles, waving in the wind to signal an event. Bright colors and simple, bold symbols lent a festive note suitable to the celebration that it advertised. Because of the temporary nature of the banner, edges were not turned. Pieces were sewn simply and quickly.

Banners came to be treasured, and today have evolved into popular wall hangings—a familiar appliqué form.

Felt is often used today as a material for banners and hangings, because parts may be secured to the background with a white glue such as Elmer's or Sobo (as may other fabrics) in preparation for sewing. White glue along the edge also prevents raveling of many fabrics and can act as a preservative for the fabric, impregnating its fibers.

Truly contemporary appliqué forms have emerged too. The fabulous new sewing machines are one source and signature of contemporary appliqué, but unique combinations of fabrics and other materials like feathers, yarns, grasses, and shells are as much a part of this art form. Transparent fabrics, fabrics rich in texture, spray dyes, metallic nonwovens, all add to your vocabulary and greatly expand the potential of the medium. Even try combining spray paint, batik, tie-dye, and other techniques with appliqué and embroidery.

A Felt Appliqué Rug

A large piece of heavy felt was first spread on the floor and a design developed by Thelma R. Newman chosen, working directly with pieces of felt.

Rather than basting or pinning, the pieces of felt to be appliquéd were held in place with a rubber cement of the type used by milliners.

The pieces of felt were then tacked in place quickly using a spread zigzag stitch that was then stitched over in satin stitch.

Felt holds up well as a floor covering. This rug in maroon, red, black, and beige felts, by Thelma R. Newman, has the qualities of a banner and could be used as a wall hanging as well.

106

A felt banner by Jane Bearman.

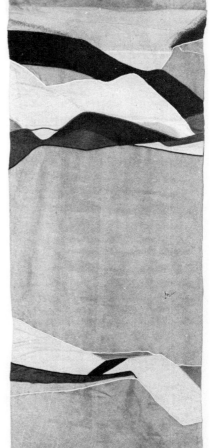

Animal Fiber X (24" x 62"), by Anna V. A. Polesný, is a hanging scroll of machine-embroidered, machine-appliquéd, and stuffed suede. Satin stitching and free-machine embroidery were used throughout the piece to strengthen and soften elements of the design. *Courtesy: Anna V. A. Polesný; photo by Anna V. A. Polesný*

Reversible Wrap Skirt with Reversible Appliqué

That appliqué is a medium of extraordinary potential is further illustrated by this reversible wrap skirt with reversible appliqué designed by Thelma R. Newman. The patterns for a branch, buds, blossoms, and leaves were sketched on heavy brown paper and then cut out. Here, the patterns are arranged on the skirt. Fabric shapes are cut in the shape of the patterns to be appliquéd.

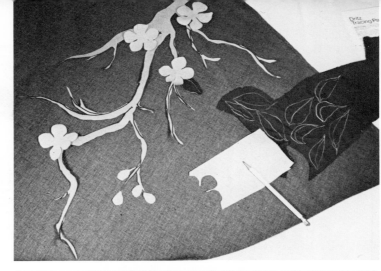

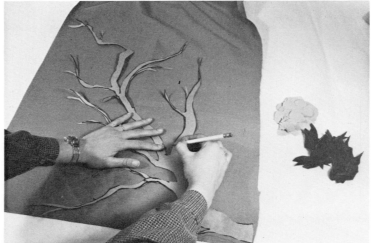

The branch is placed over a piece of fabric, traced, and the traced form cut from the fabric. Leaves, buds, and blossoms previously cut from fabrics of desired colors are at right.

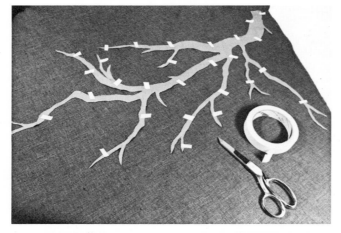

The fabric branch is carefully arranged on the skirt and held in place with masking tape.

The fabric branch is then sewn to the skirt using satin stitch. The pieces of tape are removed, as necessary during sewing. Note that the reverse side of the skirt is bunched at the right to make certain that the satin stitching does not pass through both layers.

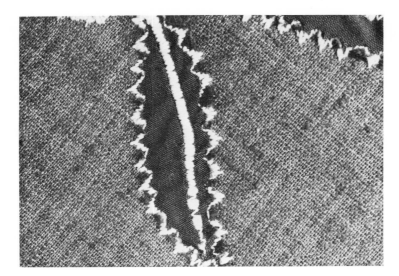

This detail shows the appliqué of a single leaf using a decorative stitch and satin stitch, attaching it securely to the skirt.

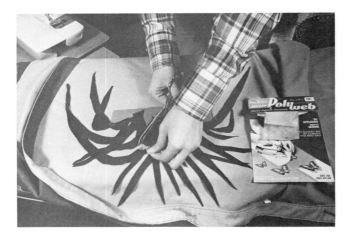

An entirely different design—a potted plant—is created for the reverse side of the skirt. Green leaves are cut directly from fabric and arranged on the reverse side of the skirt. Pieces of Poly-Web (an adhesive that bonds fabric when a hot iron is applied) are placed under the fabric leaves to secure them to the skirt as an aid in sewing.

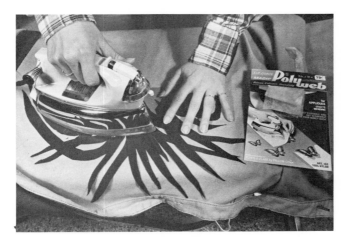

A hot iron is used to melt the Poly-Web between the fabrics and join them. The outline of each leaf is then followed in satin stitch to complete the appliqué of the top part of the pocket.

109

The bottom part of this planter pocket was also constructed with the aid of Poly-Web. Leaf and outlines and pot details are satin stitch. The pocket bottom was attached to the skirt with satin stitch, too.

The reverse side of this skirt, designed by Thelma R. Newman, shows the completed branch design.

110

Anna V. A. Polesný used
machine satin stitching as both
a decorative and structural
technique in creating this top
of suede appliqué. The skirt is
silk noil screen-printed by
hand.

A close-up of the machine-
embroidered and -appliquéd
suede top by Anna V. A
Polesný. *Photos courtesy Anna
V. A. Polesný*

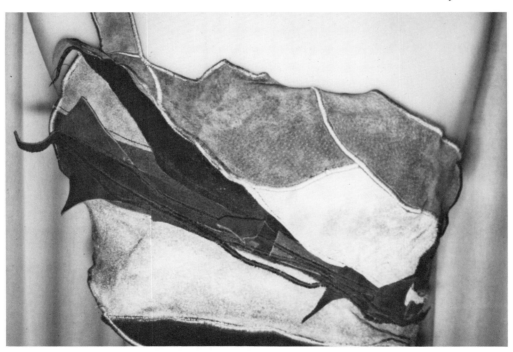

Appalachian Winter, an appliqué picture by Gloria L. Bubeck. *Courtesy: Gloria L. Bubeck*

A wall hanging by Blanche Carstenson made of transparent and opaque fabrics.

Cameo and *Country*, pillows machine-embroidered and -appliquéd by Margaret Cusack. *Courtesy: Margaret Cusack*

Bread poster, *How to Make Bread Like Grandma Used to Make*, appliqué collage by Margaret Cusack. *Courtesy: Margaret Cusack*

114

Harvest (5′ x 9′), an appliquéd hanging by Margaret Cusack commissioned by architect George Nelson. *Courtesy: Margaret Cusack; photo by eeva-inkeri*

115

Structural Appliqué: Rain Scarf of Ribbon and Plastic

When appliqué is structural as well as decorative, it becomes something more than what we generally think of as the application of fabric to fabric. In this case, a "fabric" was woven of satin ribbon and combined with clear acetate (otherwise used as a tablecloth) to create a rain scarf. The strips of satin ribbon are interwoven, arranged on an oversized piece of the clear plastic, and held in place with pieces of masking tape. The process of tacking the ribbon to the plastic is time-consuming and requires patience because the ribbon and plastic are both slippery. After tacking, the ribbon and plastic are sewn along each edge of each strip of ribbon with the featherstitch. Make certain that the plastic remains taut and does not wrinkle or pucker. The ribbon must be kept in alignment as well. Loose threads should be cut frequently. As shown, excess ribbon may be trimmed later.

Because the plastic and adhesive from the tape may build up on the needle, it is advisable to clean the needle frequently. A needle lubricant, such as Need-L-Lub®, may be useful too. After sewing, the tape may be peeled away. And remember that because needle holes will be visible in the plastic, take some time to practice accurate sewing to avoid mistakes.

A close-up of the featherstitched satin ribbon and clear acetate.

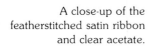

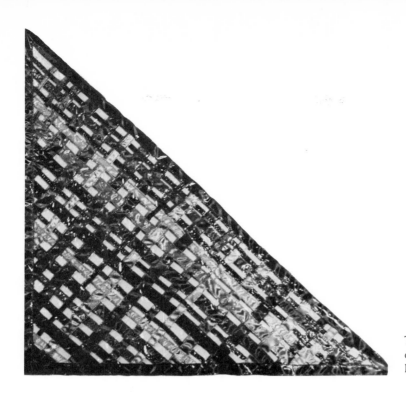

The finished rain scarf, designed by Thelma R. Newman.

A pillow machine-appliquéd with satin stitch in rich fabrics with contrasting textures, by Mountain Artisans.

Joan Schulze employed subdued colors in *Cityscape* (27″ x 19″), a
landscape in machine appliqué. *Courtesy: Joan Schulze*

Jungle Fantasy, straight-stitched and satin-stitched machine appliqué, by Andrea Aldredge. *Courtesy: Andrea Aldredge*

In many applications, appliqué will be subordinated to machine-embroidered detail. This flower illustrates the use of a variety of machine stitches to decorate appliquéd fabric.

Elaborate machine embroidery, whether on appliquéd fabric or plain fabric, is often more easily created using an embroidery hoop.

The completed appliqué-machine embroidery.

120

Fly in the Ointment, by Joan Blumenbaum, appliquéd elements enriched through the lavish use of free machine embroidery. *Courtesy: Joan Blumenbaum*

Close-up of *Fly in the Ointment* showing the elegant use of cording as an outlining material and a variety of machine-embroidery stitches by Joan Blumenbaum. *Courtesy: Joan Blumenbaum*

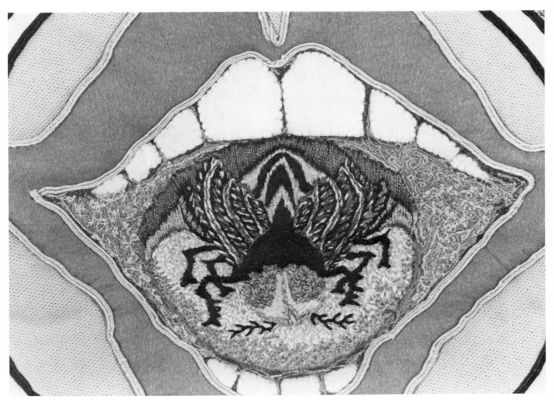

Machine Embroidery
by Mary Ball

Mary Ball uses the satin stitch to appliqué and embroider wall hangings.

A wall hanging and close-up by Mary Ball.

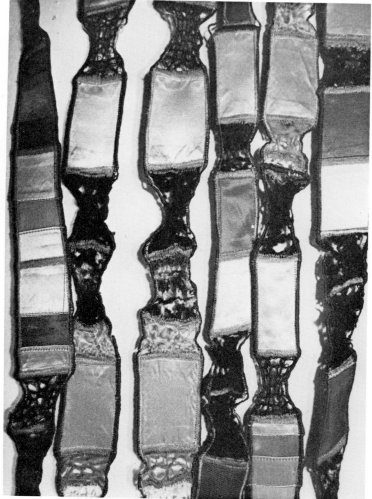

122

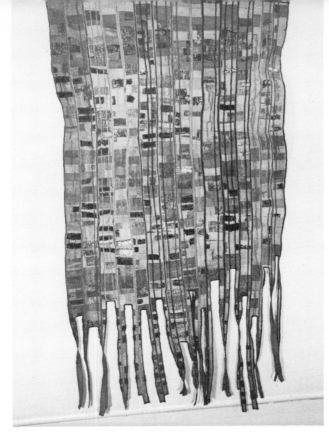

Machine-appliquéd and
-embroidered wall hangings by
Mary Ball.

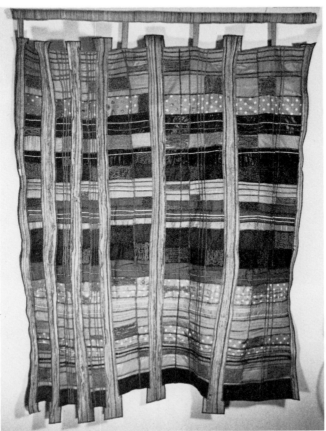

123

Sunflower Appliqué

The sunflower appliqué designed as a pocket for a sundress by Thelma R. Newman is executed in free-motion embroidery, stuffing, and appliqué. The inspiration for the appliqué was a sunflower seed packet. First the flower is sketched on paper and then resketched to scale on the fabric with tailor's chalk.

The piece of fabric is backed with interfacing as reinforcement.

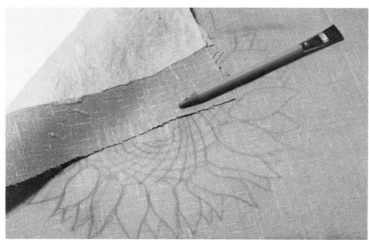

Free-motion zigzag stitching is used to fill in the center of the flower, working in a hoop without a presser foot. The overlapping lines that radiate from the center of the flower were straight-stitched with a presser foot. Yellow petals are also free-embroidered in zigzag without a presser foot.

The embroidered muslin was turned upside down on the worktable, and Poly-Fil® was placed on the underside of each petal for a three-dimensional effect.

124

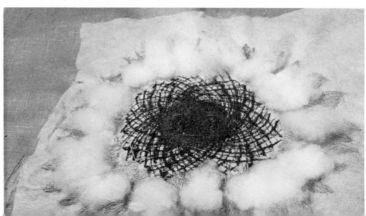

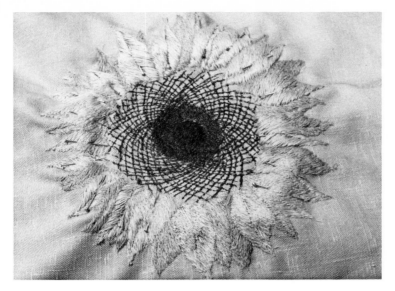

Another piece of fabric was laid over the filler and the sandwich was turned right side up to facilitate the pinning of top, filler, and bottom together. The bottom piece of fabric (which is the same as the fabric used to make the dress) will serve as a backing for sandwiching the stuffing. It will also be the lining for the dress pocket.

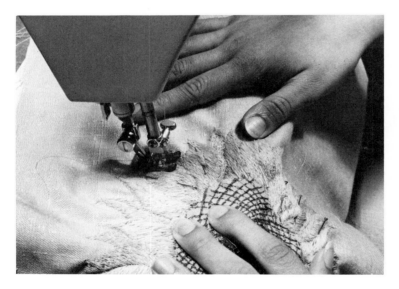

The fabric sandwich is sewn together very near the edge of the embroidery and on the outline of each petal, using a stretch stitch. To cause the petals of the sunflower to puff out, hold the backing fabric taut by stretching it during sewing. If the backing is not kept flat during sewing, the back will puff out rather than the front.

The sunflower is then cut from the fabric, with care taken to allow a thin border of fabric to remain outside the outline of stitching.

The completed sunflower, front
and back.

A dress was made from the
same material on which the
sunflower was embroidered,
and leaves to support the
sunflower were free-
embroidered on the left front
of the dress using satin stitch.
Wide stitches were used to give
a silky quality to the leaf.

Tridimensional Pellon interfacing is used behind the leaf embroidery for support. Excess interfacing is later cut away from the inside of the dress.

The sunflower is sewn onto the dress above the free-embroidered leaves. It is stitched to the dress only two-thirds of the way around its perimeter, to allow it to be used as a pocket.

In *The Point*, Bets Ramsey appliqués fabrics with various textures and uses free-machine embroidery to create a landscape with mystical qualities. *Courtesy: Bets Ramsey; photo by T. Fred Muller*

127

Marilyn (20" x 25"), appliquéd and stuffed collage by Margaret Cusack. *Courtesy: Margaret Cusack*

128

4

QUILTING, PATCHWORK,
TRAPUNTO, AND
STUFFED FORMS

Quilting, patchwork, trapunto, and stuffing are techniques for creating three-dimensional effects with fabric and constructing fabric into relief and sculptural forms. All these techniques have traditionally involved hand sewing alone, but machine sewing can be used to replace laborious hand-sewing operations without sacrificing aesthetics in the least. For the most part, the techniques remain the same when a sewing machine is employed, except that the machine speeds each process. The special features many machines offer may add a new dimension to these sculptural processes.

QUILTING

Quilting is a very old technique in which a layer (or layers) of filler (batting, wadding, or stuffing) is sandwiched between pieces of fabric. The sandwich of fabric and filler may be held together by stitching or by rows of knots. Either method will throw the fabric into shallow relief. The quilted relief effect is extremely attrac-

In *The Couple*, by Elizabeth Gurrier, human forms (heads, arms, and feet) are integrated into a quilt made of ribless corduroy with stitching in wool, cotton, and metallic thread. The hair is unspun wool. Both machine and hand stitching were used for construction and quilting. *Courtesy: Elizabeth S. Gurrier*

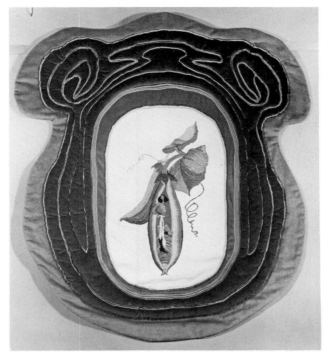

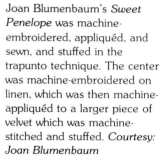

Joan Blumenbaum's *Sweet Penelope* was machine-embroidered, appliquéd, and sewn, and stuffed in the trapunto technique. The center was machine-embroidered on linen, which was then machine-appliquéd to a larger piece of velvet which was machine-stitched and stuffed. *Courtesy: Joan Blumenbaum*

A close-up of the machine-embroidered woman in peapod, the centerpiece of *Sweet Penelope* by Joan Blumenbaum. *Courtesy: Joan Blumenbaum*

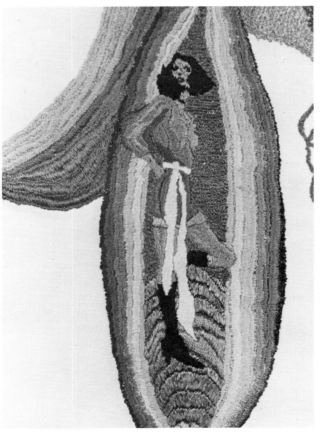

tive, but also serves a practical purpose. Fabrics were originally quilted to provide a greater amount of warmth for their weight, as blankets or as clothing. Medieval knights used quilted underwear to ward off the chill of armor and prevent metal from chafing against their skin.

Functional origins have long since given way to the aesthetic, and quilting has been used for everything from blankets to petticoats, pillows, rugs, potholders, toys, upholstery and shopping bags.

Quilts usually have three layers: a top layer of fabric, a middle layer of batting, and a bottom layer of fabric.

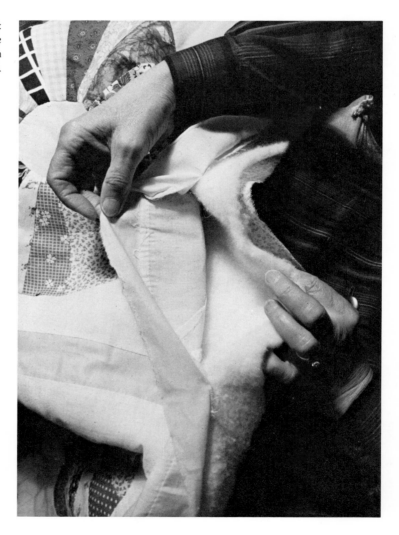

132

HAND-BASTING PATTERN AND DIRECTION BEFORE QUILTING

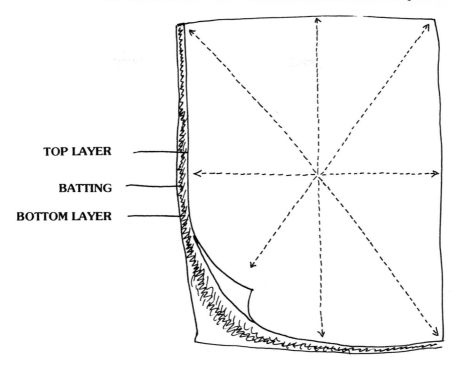

TOP LAYER

BATTING

BOTTOM LAYER

MACHINE QUILTING—DIRECTION AND SEQUENCE FOR DIAMOND PATTERN

After the layers of the quilt have been assembled, but before the quilt is set into a hoop for sewing, the layers are held together with hand basting. The top diagram describes the direction and position of basting used in hand quilting. The bottom diagram illustrates the directions and sequence to be used both in basting and sewing for machine quilting in a diamond pattern.

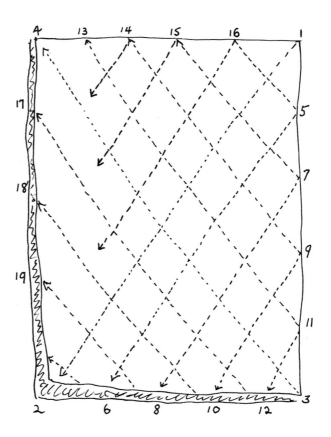

MAKING A BASIC QUILT

The technique for making a basic quilt is essentially the same whether the quilt is to be made by hand or with the aid of a machine. There are several distinct advantages to using a machine in quilting. The advantages are speed and an expanded range of stitches. A machine makes it possible to use specialty stitches, such as the satin stitch, that would otherwise be extremely impractical to use in quilting. It is possible to design quilts around particular types of stitches, or at least to include special stitches, rather than rely solely upon the running straight stitch (the traditional quilter's stitch). A possible limitation on machine quilting should, however, be noted. If a quilt is large it may be difficult to sew intricate patterns by machine—a point to keep in mind when planning your design.

MATERIALS

Materials for a basic quilt consist of a top layer of fabric, a layer (or layers) of filler, a lining (fabric for the underside of the quilt) and accessories for implementation of the quilt design. The top fabric may be almost any kind of textile that is smooth, soft, preshrunk, and, preferably, colorfast. Heavy, stiff fabrics are difficult to quilt and do not easily form a design in relief. Closely woven fabrics, which are difficult to quilt by hand because they require a great deal of effort to penetrate with a hand-held needle, often may be quilted effectively by machine.

The bottom fabric (the backing or lining) should be of a loose weave such as India cloth, muslin, monk's cloth, cotton, or linen. Remove selvages so that they will not cause puckering later.

The filler is usually batting of some kind. Cotton or preferably Dacron/polyester are most frequently used. Felt, terry cloth, wool (particularly old woolen blankets that have been washed), flannel, foam rubber or polyurethane foam, down, and kapok are used with success, too. The newest polyester fillers are probably the easiest to work with because they are lightweight, lie flat, wash well, and tend not to mat together as easily as other fillers, such as certain cottons. Loose fillers such as down and kapok tend to shift within their quilted spaces unless only very small distances are allowed to remain between the quilting stitches. Such fillers are more appropriate for stuffed forms, as discussed below.

A binding for the edges of the quilt will be needed also. A bias binding is usually used for quilts. It may be purchased ready-made or made from the same fabric that is used for the top or lining of the quilt.

Other essential materials include a sharp four-inch or six-inch scissors. When quilts are hand-sewn, number 40–60 quilting thread or, for very fine fabric, number 80 quilting thread is used. When quilts are sewn by machine, number 80 thread is usually employed. Dacron-covered cotton threads are very strong and work well.

PATTERNS FOR QUILTING

Templates are usually used for hand quilting, with the quilt often being sewn directly around the template. Of course, quilting designs can also be drawn with pencil or chalk directly on the fabric (before or after it has been assembled and basted). A tracing wheel or pin can also be used to make holes in tracing paper so that chalk can be forced through the holes onto the fabric to transfer the pattern for quilting ("prick and pounce"—see Chapter 2).

Straight lines of stitching can be used to form diamonds, squares, and rectangles. Such shapes may be overlapped to create new shapes and patterns. Circles also can be repeated and overlapped to create shapes and border designs. French curves may be used to form feather shapes, scallops, clam shells, and so forth. In short, many shapes may be used to create designs for quilting. Many techniques may be used to transfer designs for quilting to the fabric to be quilted. The method you use will depend upon what feels most com-

135

fortable. Bear in mind that special stitches and variations of traditional stitches have an important place in machine quilting. The satin stitch is especially versatile, because its width can be varied so easily. The feather-stitch and twin needle stitches should also be considered as elements of your design vocabulary.

THE PROCEDURE FOR QUILTING

On a clean, level surface large enough to spread out your fabric (such as a table or a floor), spread the lining wrong side up (with right side facing down). Place one or two thicknesses of batting over the entire lining, edge to edge to edge. Then place the fabric, top side up, over the batting. Each layer should lie smooth and flat. Next, with a running stitch (using number 50 or number 60 thread in eighteen-inch lengths) baste the three layers together starting from the center and radiating outward toward the corners. Take care to catch all layers with every stitch. Basting stitches should generally be approximately four to six inches apart. This basting will be removed later, but, at least temporarily, it will function to hold lining, batting, and fabric together and to keep them from shifting.

Up until this point, the procedures for hand quilting and for machine quilting have been the same, but, since we will quilt by machine, the procedure for machine quilting will be described. To prepare the machine for machine quilting, remove the presser foot and set the pressure to darning or zero. Place your fabric in a large embroidery or quilting hoop and begin stitching in the pattern you have chosen. To begin, try a simple diamond pattern. Sew diagonally across the fabric first in one direction and then in the other (beginning in the center and radiating out toward the edges). Remember that, since the pressure is not being regulated, you must make certain that the stitches are of uniform tightness. If you are using a hoop, be certain it is not too large; otherwise the hoop may constrain the length of the stitched line, because the body of the machine may get in the way. Hoops are especially good for circular patterns and finely detailed quilting.

CARE OF QUILTS

Before washing a quilt, be certain that all materials (filler, thread, and coverings) are colorfast and shrinkproof. Wash by machine in cold water with a mild cold-water detergent, such as Woolite®, using a short cycle. A half cup of white vinegar added to the wash cycle acts as a mild fixative and will help to keep colors from washing out. Dry your quilt either on a clothesline or by tumbling with *cool* air. Never press a quilt with an iron, and never wash a quilt that has a wool filler. The best method of cleaning a quilt is through a French dry-cleaning process—but not by the regular mechanical dry cleaning method, which may destroy the quilting stitches.

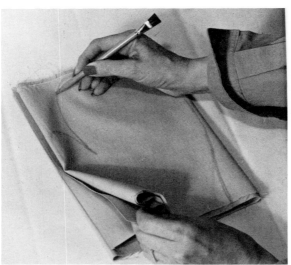

Quilted Kitchen Mitts

These quilted mitts were constructed of eight layers of broadcloth and a layer of polyester batting to provide insulation from hot pans and dishes. A sheet of fabric is folded over itself three times to create eight layers of fabric. The general outline of the back of the right-hand mitt is then sketched on the fabric in tailor's chalk.

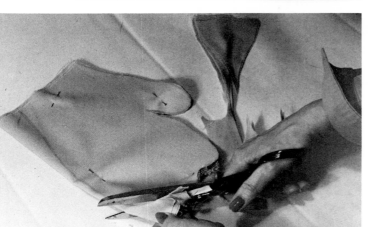

The eight-layer mitt is cut along the sketched outline.

137

The outline of the design to be sewn (as well as the pattern for quilting) on the back of the right-hand mitt is sketched in tailor's chalk. The fabric with the sketch is then placed over another piece of fabric (the piece that would serve as the palm of the right-hand mitt). The two pieces are laid over a sheet of dressmaker's carbon (with the carbon side facing up) and the design is traced using a tracing wheel.

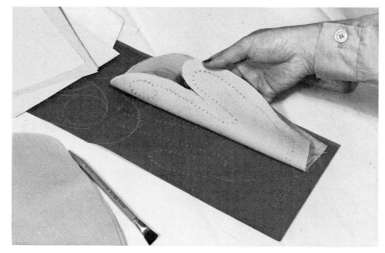

The tracing transfers the mirror image of the design for the back of the mitt to the palm of the mitt, as illustrated.

The same procedure is followed in creating a left-hand mitt. Mitt backs and palms shown after sketching and tracing.

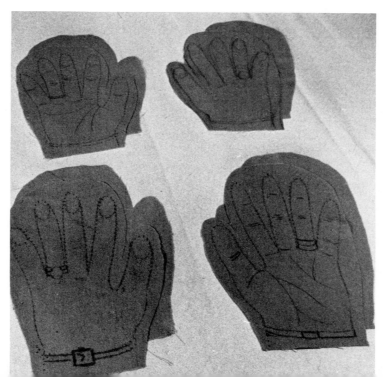

138

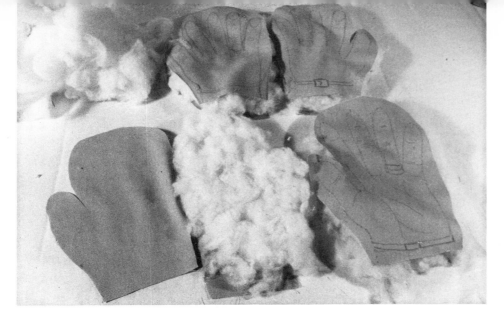

In preparation for sewing, place batting between the two top layers and the two bottom layers of fabric that would form the back and palm of each mitt. Polyester batting is used here.

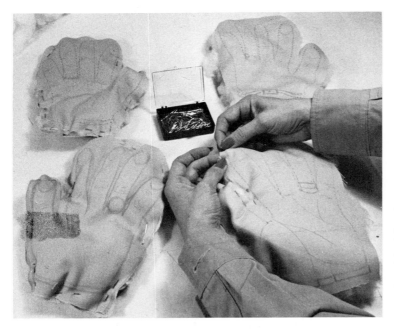

Pin each back and palm section in preparation for sewing. In designing a mitt, considerable thought should be given to the ultimate size because not only do quilting and batting make the mitt "smaller" because of the puffiness, but an allowance must be made for the seam created when the back and palm of each mitt are sewn together.

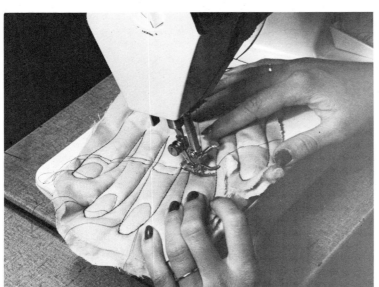

Each section is machine-quilted along the hand outline using the stretch stitch. It is a good idea to practice stitching over stuffing before beginning work on the final form. It is much easier to stitch over a thick layer of stuffing if you compress fabric and stuffing as you feed it under the presser foot. Line details were added in straight stitch.

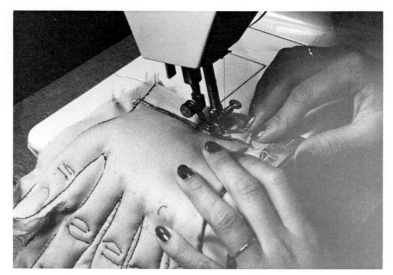

Watch, bracelet, and rings were satin-stitched with metallic thread. Because the material was puffy, no attempt was made to cover with the satin stitch on the first pass. Rather, two passes were made.

Bits of colored material were appliquéd (with an added bit of batting underneath) to create "rings" on two fingers. Several passes with the zigzag stitch were used to create the satin-stitch effect, with metallic thread.

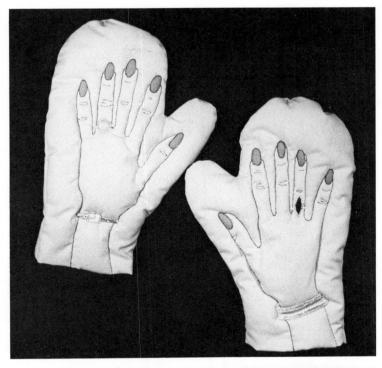

In the finished "Hand" mitts, designed by Thelma R. Newman, the nails were colored using textile markers.

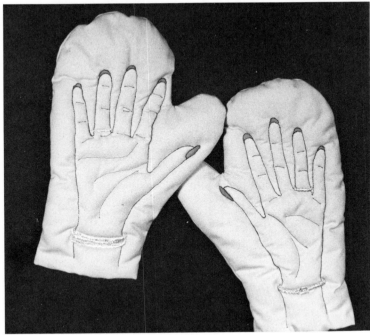

A silk satin pillow (18″ x 20″) in trapunto with machine quilting in silk
thread by Sandra Ward. *Courtesy: Sandra Ward*

A machine-quilted box by Margaret Cusack.

There is more to Sara Drower's wall hanging, *Biology 101 Quilt*, than meets the eye. The five sections shown are part of a much larger piece. Old laboratory drawings were redone (with humor) in paint and permanent dye on unbleached cotton muslin. After quilting, the amoeba in the upper left-hand corner was super-stuffed from the back in the trapunto technique. The inclusions are glass beads that were stitched on by hand. Next to the amoeba is a paramecium, also outlined in black machine quilting, with hand-knotted cilia along its edge. Euglena, at the top right, sports a whiplike flagellum of black satin.

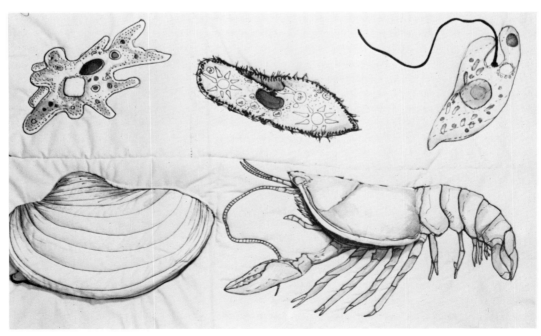

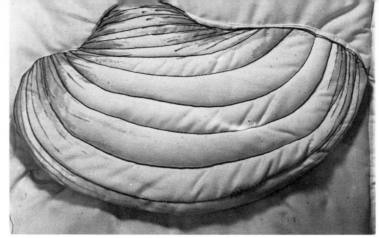

The clamshell was lightly quilted following its natural lines. Only its top edge was appliquéd to the hanging so that it would open to reveal . . .

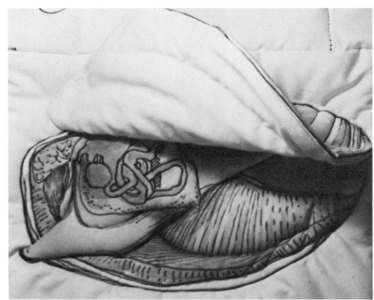

. . . Sara Drower's painting of a clam also embroidered, quilted, and stuffed in parts in the trapunto technique. Sara Drower prefers to use cotton or polyester thread and fairly small stitches. Because her designs require constant guiding and turning during machine sewing she prefers to work in sections and then assemble the pieces, as she did in *Biology 101 Quilt.*

The crayfish's carapace, like the clam's shell, was quilted lightly and may be lifted to reveal a machine-quilted drawing. Each leg and claw was machine-quilted too.

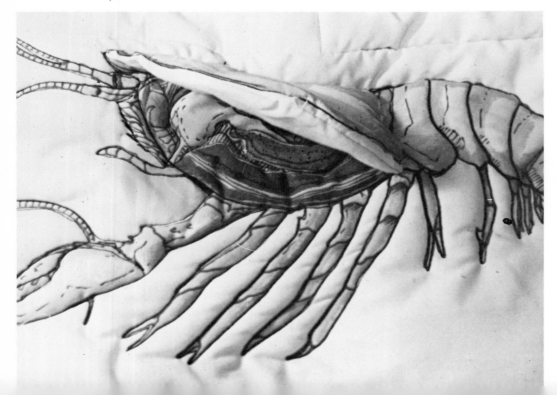

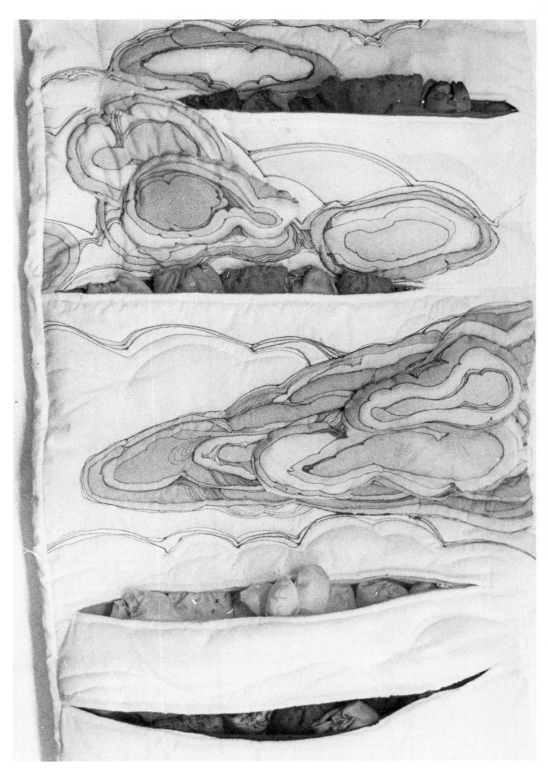

Secret Rainbow (24″ x 80″), by Sara Drower, is a cotton wall hanging with
treasure pockets. Sara Drower begins by painting and drawing on the   145
fabric to be quilted, sets the dyes, and uses large sheets of polyester
batting.

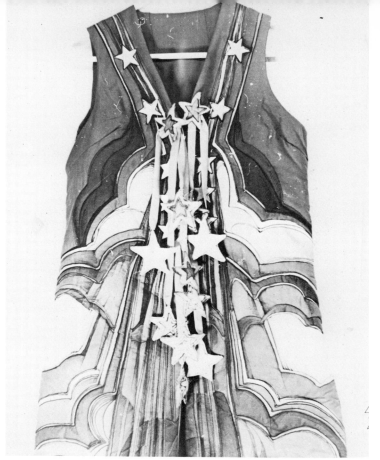

Sara Drower's *Cosmic Vest* is lightly quilted; each cloud and star is outlined in black machine straight stitching.

A close-up of Sara Drower's machine-quilted *Cosmic Vest. All photos courtesy Sara Drower*

A close-up of a quilt designed by Charles Counts and executed by Rising Fawn Quilters, showing the pattern of machine quilting.

Nine Dancing Girls (54" x 32"), a wall quilt, by Lenore Davis. The design is painted on cotton velveteen with Procion ® fiber-reactive dyes. After painting, the fabric is machine-quilted over a layer of filler with a muslin backing. Legs, bras, and faces are stuffed with additional polyester filler, to increase the relief, by slitting the muslin backing, inserting filler, and closing the slits by hand sewing. The entire piece is edged with cotton velveteen on the bias to create a ½" border. *Courtesy: Lenore Davis*

147

PATCHWORK

Patchwork—fabric created by piecing together small pieces of other fabrics—is often thought of in the context of quilting because the patchwork quilt is so widely known and admired. But patchwork fabrics are used in many different applications, including tablecloths, draperies, clothing, lampshades, and wall hangings, to name only a few.

DESIGNING PATCHWORK

Traditional patchwork often involves designs based on geometric shapes: triangles, squares, circles, and rectangles. But, as the "crazy" patchwork quilts suggest, patchwork is hardly limited to such designs and is particularly responsive to individual inspiration.

The best way to design a patchwork quilt may be to carefully plot your design in full scale on a sheet of kraft paper. Patchwork should always be designed with careful attention to the interplay of light and dark forms. Dark and light patches should form patterns and patterns within patterns as well. After sketching, the next step is to create templates around which fabric patches will be cut. Patterns may be made of the same kraft paper on which the overall pattern was sketched. Templates made of heavier materials such as oaktag (a lightweight cardboard used for posters), sandpaper, cardboard, plastic, masonite, or metal are often used to cut patches—particularly in geometric designs that require many patches of the same size and shape.

CUTTING THE PATCHES

The patterns or templates from which patches will be cut should be slightly larger than the dimensions of the patch to allow for seams. An allowance of one-fourth of an inch per seam should be sufficient.

In preparation for cutting pieces of fabric, carefully press the fabric so that there are no wrinkles. Always use fabrics of the best quality that you can afford. A great deal of effort goes into quilt-making, and better fabrics will last longer. Firm weaves are best. Percales are particularly good and should have 120 (or at least 80) threads per inch. Colors should be fast and all fabrics should be preshrunk. Calicos, ginghams, satins, percales, wools, silks, velvets, and tightly woven linens work well, producing luxurious patchwork. Of course, polyester and cotton blends are effective too.

When possible, place your template on the fabric so that the warp and weft of the fabric are parallel to sides of the template. Draw around the template with a pencil, and cut the fabric accurately with sharp scissors. Be certain to cut your corners sharply as well. You may then trace a seam line one-fourth inch from the edge of each side of each patch, or simply use a seam gauge or mark on your sewing machine to maintain even and accurate seams.

PIECING THE PATCHWORK

Most patchworks, unless they are small and involve very few patches, are constructed from blocks of patchwork. To sew patches together into blocks, set the top-thread tension at universal (normal) and the stitch length at twenty stitches per inch. A one-quarter-inch seam may be maintained using the line gauge found on most machines. Begin by sewing patches together to form a row, then sew several rows together to form a block. The blocks themselves may be sewn together to create a larger piece.

As in quilting, borders are sewn last. Their width can vary considerably, corners may be mitered, and borders may be wider at the top than at the bottom.

Ultrasuede Patchwork Skirt and Pillow

Patchwork is most often associated with quilting, but patchwork need not be quilted at all. This patchwork fabric of Ultrasuede scraps was assembled and used in a long skirt and pillow. Scraps of blue, cream, and tan Ultrasuede were trimmed, overlapped, pinned, and sewn with zigzag stitch. In order to create a patchwork that will lie flat, pin and sew the pieces one at a time. Do not attempt to pin many pieces and sew them all at once, because in patchwork the pieces often shift and stretch, and as a result may pucker if you pin and sew too many at once. Ultrasuede is easy to use in patchwork because it has no grain.

To complete the patchwork Ultrasuede dress, a waistband was attached and the bottom was finished by trimming it to the proper length—no hem was needed. The fabric and the skirt were designed by Thelma R. Newman.

150

Ultrasuede pillows with a corded edge were made from the same patchwork fabric.

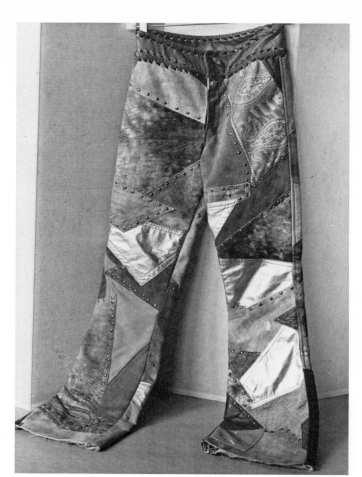

Smithskin Clothes made these slacks in a patchwork of suede overstitched by machine and decorated with metal rivets.

Diane Herrick-Kvistad's machine-stitched patchwork vest in a symmetrical pattern reverses to blue corduroy. *Courtesy: Diane Herrick-Kvistad*

152

Karen's Quilt, by Joy Saville, is a patchwork quilt in corduroys and velvets. *Courtesy: Joy Saville*

Joy Saville's *Supernova* (38" x 48") is a patchwork quilt in an original design. She quilted the patchwork in concentric circles radiating outward from the center. *Courtesy: Joy Saville; photos by Jack Young*

Woman at Sea (37" x 48"), a
patchwork quilt by Joy Saville.
*Courtesy: Joy Saville; photos
by Jack Young*

A Rainbow is Shelter, machine-appliquéd and -quilted wall hanging by Andrea Aldredge. *Courtesy: Andrea Aldredge*

TRAPUNTO AND STUFFED FORMS

Many of the pieces included in this book combine the techniques of machine embroidery, appliqué, quilting, and patchwork with trapunto and stuffed work. It is solely for descriptive puposes that trapunto and stuffing are discussed separately.

Stuffing is, simply stated, a technique for creating three-dimensional fabric forms. Quilting is one form of stuffed fabric, but stuffed work may move far beyond quilting. Large, intricate forms may be created using wads of cotton batting, wool, kapok, feathers, down, foam rubber, polyurethane foam, latex, rags, or even beans, rice, or expanded polystyrene pellets to give fabric shape. As the qualities of the various materials referred to above might suggest, stuffed forms may feel very different—some may be soft, light, and fluffy, others hard, rigid, and dense. Because each filler has unique characteristics, careful consideration should be given to the choice of a stuffing material. Elaborate embroidered patterns and appliqué may be executed prior to finally stuffing a project.

Trapunto is a specialized kind of stuffed form. High relief is created by stuffing channels between two layers of cloth with filler. The layers of cloth may be sewn together with a straight or a decorative stitch. The top layer may be a fancy or decorated fabric while the bottom layer will often be a fabric with a slightly loose weave such as muslin or linen. To stuff the channels, the weave of the bottom layer is usually spread apart so that stuffing material can be forced into the space to be filled and thereby projected into relief. The backing that had been spread is then moved back to its original position. When the backing will not be visible in the finished piece, it may even be slit to allow stuffing and then be stitched closed by hand. Stuffing can also be pushed into the channels from the edges of the fabric. But pushing stuffing in from behind, through the backing, is often more convenient and easier because the density of the stuffing and the detail to be formed in relief can be more readily controlled. Trapunto has many variants. In Florentine trapunto, for instance, three layers of fabric are often used: a backing, a top lining, and a sheer, semitransparent material such as a silk or an organdy over the top lining. The top lining may also be decorated with drawings or in stitchery. Colored yarn or other fillers also may be used between the top lining and the top fabric to create yet other effects.

COMBINED TECHNIQUES

Much of the work in this book combines several techniques. Machine embroidery (as distinguished from machine stitching) is nearly always used in appliqué and in quilting, and often is used in creating patchwork.

Stuffed forms and trapunto pieces frequently will be decorated primarily with machine stitching. Our parting pitch is for you always to keep the entire range of embroidery techniques in mind when designing and to experiment with them freely in order to experience the joys of creating exciting and original forms using machine stitchery and embroidery.

Forms can be partially quilted or stuffed as well. In *Can the Great-Crested Grebe Grin?* (19" x 19"), Joan Blumenbaum appliquéd the felt lips to their background over polyester stuffing to make them stand out.

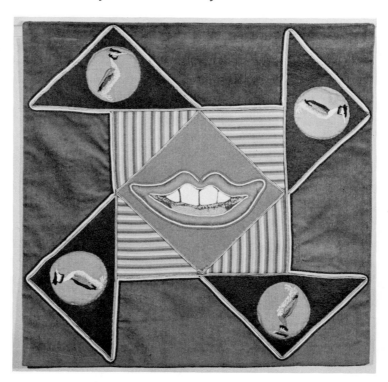

The lips are outlined in machine-sewn cording and are an example of filled free embroidery.

Joan Blumenbaum's bird motif was hand-embroidered, lightly stuffed, and sewn to a felt triangle that was appliquéd to the larger background. *Courtesy: Joan Blumenbaum; photos by Joan Blumenbaum*

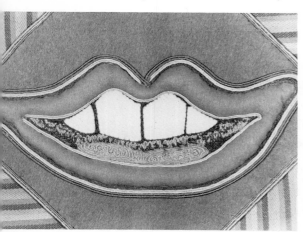

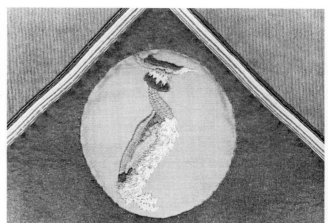

Tina Bobker and Carol
Dlugasch used a similar
technique in creating these wall
hangings. Each picture is
constructed in machine-sewn
appliqué and is then given a
quilted look by placing batting
behind important areas and
outlining the areas with
additional stitching. Each
picture is then framed in soft,
stuffed fabric. *Courtesy: Tina
Bobker and Carol Dlugasch,
Rainbow Artisans, Inc.*

Lee Newman began by sketching another toothsome design in marking pen and executed it in a unique way.

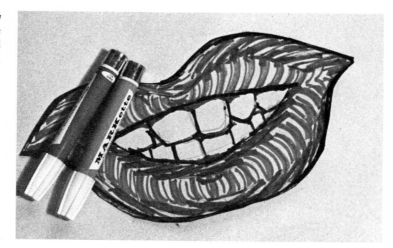

He machine-embroidered adhesive-backed metallic Mylar film with red thread, stuffed the lips from behind with polyester filler, and mounted the machine-embroidered stuffed plastic on a piece of black acrylic.

Trapunto is similar to quilting. In quilting the stuffing is sewn into place, whereas in trapunto the space is defined by stitching first and adding the stuffing later. The latter technique allows for much greater flexibility in achieving depth and variation in form. *Eve's Tree* (16″ x 12″), a trapunto pillow by Doreen Lah, was machine-stitched and stuffed from behind through a muslin backing. *Courtesy: Doreen Lah*

In *Stained Glass* (16″ x 16″), another pillow by Doreen Lah, parts are trapunto and parts are quilted. Cording was machine-sewn and beads were added by hand. *Courtesy: Doreen Lah*

Night Lady (60″ x 48″), by Josephine Schwartz, was executed in machine-stitched suede appliqué and trapunto.

Machine-stitched appliqué and trapunto wall hanging (54″ x 36″) by Josephine Schwartz. *Courtesy: Josephine Schwartz*

163

Soft sculpture of stuffed
machine- and hand-sewn
muslin with crochet in white
wool by Sydel Ackerman.
Courtesy: Sydel Ackerman

Lily of the Flower is a painting in hand and machine embroidery and trapunto by Joan Blumenbaum. After sewing the channels by machine, the organdy backing was slit, in appropriate places, stuffing was inserted, and the slits closed with hand stitching. The trapunto centerpiece was appliquéd to its immediate background with hand stitching and that ground was machine-appliquéd to the darker background.

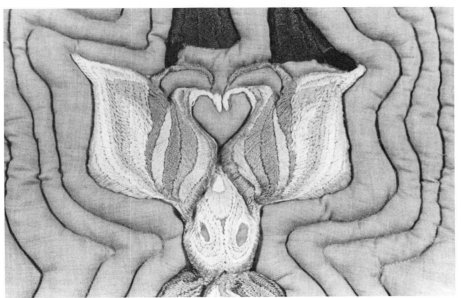

A close-up of the lily. *Courtesy: Joan Blumenbaum*

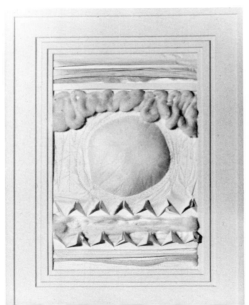

Becky King's *White Moon* (16″ x 22″) was constructed of machine-sewn paper, rolled and machine-sewn tissue paper, trapuntoed tissue paper, and machine-couched, unspun roving. *Courtesy: Becky King*

165

Two pillows (each 14″ x 14″) in machine-stitched muslin trapunto by Sydel Ackerman. *Courtesy: Sydel Ackerman*

Fragments (42" x 78"), by
Sydel Ackerman, machine-
stitched muslin trapunto panels
joined in eggshell-colored wool
crochet. *Collection of The
Morris Museum of Arts &
Sciences; courtesy: Sydel
Ackerman*

Detail of "cat" panel from
Fragments by Sydel Ackerman.
Courtesy: Sydel Ackerman

167

Sandra Ward machine-stitched and trapuntoed silk satin to create *Ascension* (54" long).

Odalisque (21" x 16"), machine-stitched silk satin trapunto by Sandra Ward.

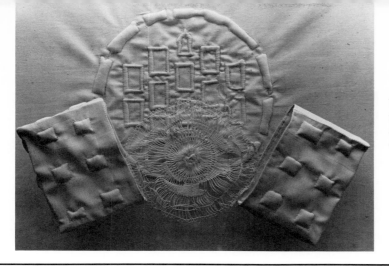

Two Worlds, a soft sculpture in machine stitching, trapunto, and macramé by Joan Schulze. *Courtesy: Joan Schulze*

A Basic Stuffed Box by Sas Colby

To construct a soft fabric box, individual envelopes of fabric are made for each side. Cardboard is used as a template.

Another template is used to trace a guideline ¼″ from each edge, and the fabric envelopes are stitched together by machine on three sides. Six envelopes are necessary for the box. The stitching is rounded at the corners.

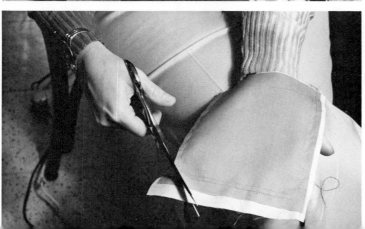

The rounded corners are clipped to the contour so that they will turn evenly without bunching when turned right side out.

169

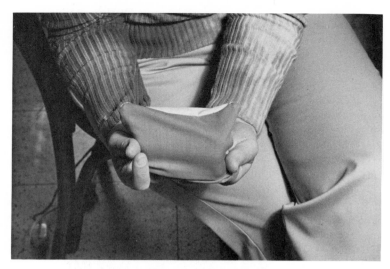

Sas Colby turns the envelope right side out, making certain that the corners are fully and evenly turned and rounded.

Small squares of fabric are then arranged in a light-dark-light-dark pattern . . .

. . . and the pieces are sewn together by machine using the straight stitch to create a small patchwork which will become part of the fabric envelope that will serve as the lid to the soft stuffed box.

170

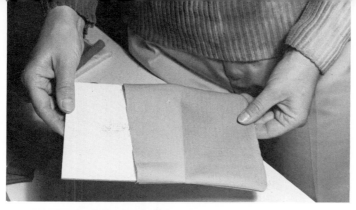

A piece of cardboard slightly smaller than the piece used as a template to mark the seam guidelines is placed inside each fabric envelope.

Sas Colby uses a knitting needle to carefully push stuffing into the corners (and throughout) the envelope on each side of the cardboard. The bottom part of the bottom panel is not stuffed, however, so that the box will sit flat without wobbling.

After having been individually stuffed, the fourth side of each stuffed envelope is closed by hand, using an invisible hemming stitch.

The stuffed envelopes are attached with straight pins to form a cube, in preparation for being sewn together. The four sides of the bottom are stitched first, then each side is sewn, all by hand using a running stitch.

After stuffing the lid, the open side is pinned closed and sewn. The lid is sewn at that edge to one edge of the top of the box so that it may be flipped open and shut.

Sas Colby's completed box with patchwork top.

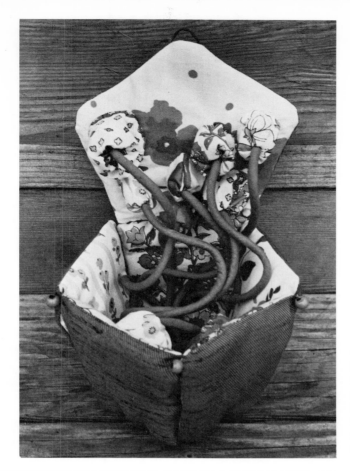

As this soft stuffed fabric box in the shape of a pentagon is opened, interior "flowers" grow. The sides of this box by Marcia Morse are not sewn together, but unbutton to reveal more wonders within.
Courtesy: Marcia Morse

Close Encounters (16″ x 48″), by Doreen Lah, is an interdigitating sculpture of machine-embroidered, appliquéd, and sewn fabrics.
Courtesy: Doreen Lah

Save the Last Waltz for Me
(10″ high, 10″ deep), another
interdigitating machine-
appliquéd and sewn sculpture
in two pieces by Doreen Lah.
Courtesy: Doreen Lah

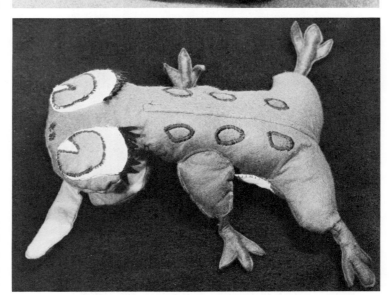

Wide Mouth Frog, by Lee
Newman, is a friendly felt
fellow decorated and
constructed entirely with
machine stitching (satin and
straight) and stuffed with
polyester fiber. Wire embedded
in the stuffing within the limbs,
spine, and tongue permits
them to be positioned.

174

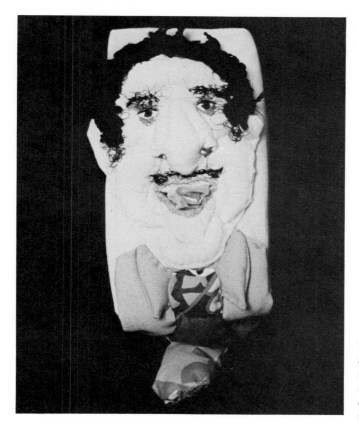

Barbara F. Lambert's hand- and machine-stitched stuffed muslin faces cover standard-size tissue boxes. Tissues are dispensed through their mouths. *Courtesy: Barbara F. Lambert*

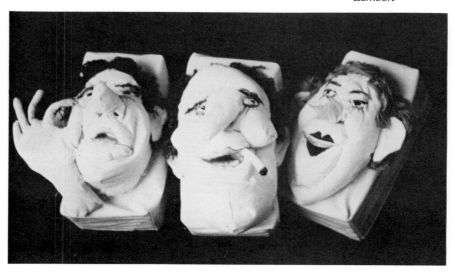

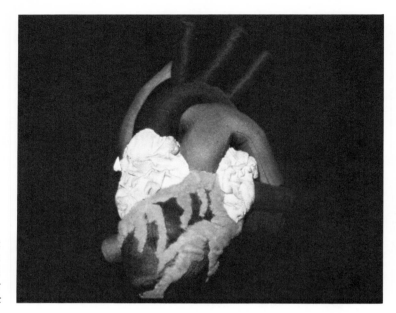

Margaret Cusack's soft heart was hand- and machine-sewn and -embroidered of felt and fabric and stuffed. *Courtesy: Margaret Cusack*

A soft sculpture woman (24" high) by Margaret Cusack is a masterpiece involving elaborate construction by hand and machine, combining appliqué and embroidery, as well as painting, stuffing, and the use of carefully selected baubles. *Courtesy: Margaret Cusack*

176

BIBLIOGRAPHY

Birrell, Verla. *The Textile Arts.* New York: Harper & Brothers, 1959.

Brightbill, Dorothy. *Quilting as a Hobby.* New York: Bonanza Books, 1973.

Butler, Anne. *Embroidery Stitches.* New York: Frederick A. Praeger, 1968.

———. *Machine Stitches.* London: B. T. Batsford Ltd., 1976.

Colby, Averil. *Quilting.* New York: Charles Scribner's Sons, 1971.

Dean, Beryl. *Creative Appliqué.* New York: Watson-Guptill Publications, 1970.

Dillmont, Thérèse de. *Encyclopedia of Needlework.* Mulhouse, France: Editions Th. de Dillmont, 1971.

Fanning, Robbie. *Decorative Machine Stitchery.* New York: Butterick Publishing, 1976.

Green, Sylvia. *Patchwork for Beginners.* New York: Watson-Guptill Publications, 1972.

Ickis, Marguerite. *The Standard Book of Quilt Making and Collecting.* New York: Dover Publications, 1959.

Laury, Jean Ray. *Appliqué Stitchery.* New York: Van Nostrand Reinhold Co., 1966.

Lillow, Ira. *Introducing Machine Embroidery.* New York: Watson-Guptill Publications, 1967.

McKim, Ruby Short. *One Hundred and One Patchwork Patterns.* New York: Dover Publications, 1962.

Marston, Doris E. *Patchwork Today.* Newton, Massachusetts: Charles T. Branford Co., 1968.

Martens, Rachel. *Modern Patchwork.* Philadelphia's Countryside Press, 1970.

Murray, Aileen. *Design in Fabric and Thread.* New York: Watson-Guptill Publications, 1969.

Museum of Contemporary Crafts, New York, catalog. *Fabric Collage.* New York: 1965.

————. *Sewn, Stitched and Stuffed.* New York: 1973.

Newman, Thelma R. *Leather as Art and Craft.* New York: Crown Publishers, Inc., 1973.

————. *Quilting, Patchwork, Appliqué, and Trapunto.* New York: Crown Publishers, Inc., 1974.

Newman, Thelma R., and Jay Hartley Newman. *The Container Book.* New York: Crown Publishers, Inc., 1977.

Passadore, Wanda. *The Needlework Book.* New York: Simon and Schuster, 1969.

Shears, Evangeline, and Diantha Fielding. *Appliqué.* New York: Watson-Guptill Publications, 1972.

Swift, Gay. *Machine Stitchery.* London: B. T. Batsford Ltd., 1974.

Wigginton, Eliot. *The Foxfire Book.* New York: Doubleday & Company, Inc., 1972.

Wooster, Ann-Sargent. *Quiltmaking.* New York: Drake Publishers, Inc., 1972.

INDEX

Numbers in italics indicate pictures.

179

INDEX